A London Christmas

Compiled by Marina Cantacuzino

ALAN SUTTON

First published in the United Kingdom in 1989
Alan Sutton Publishing Limited, Brunswick Road,
Gloucester

First published in the United States of America in 1990
Alan Sutton Publishing Inc., Wolfeboro Falls,
NH 03896–0848

British Library Cataloguing in Publication Data

A London Christmas.
1. English literature. Special subjects:
Christmas – Anthologies
I. Cantacuzino, Marina
820.8′033

ISBN 0–86299–641–1

Library of Congress Cataloging in Publication Data
applied for

Cover illustration: Caught in a Snowstorm,
Anonymous (Fine Art Photographs.)

Typesetting and origination by
Alan Sutton Publishing Limited.
Printed in Great Britain by
WBC, Bridgend, Mid Glam.

from

A London Child of the Seventies

M. VIVIAN HUGHES

In her preface to the trilogy A London Family, *M. Vivian Hughes describes herself as coming from an ordinary, suburban family 'undistinguished ourselves and unacquainted with distinguished people'. The Christmas she describes, therefore, is typical of any middle-class Victorian family of that era. Along with four older brothers she was brought up by a father who worked on the Stock Exchange, and a mother whose great extravagance was a drive in Hyde Park. Her memories run from 1870 when the family moved into a big house in Canonbury, until 1890 when she lived in Barnet with her husband and three sons.*

Nowadays it is difficult to realize that no Christmas preparations were made until the week before the day itself. All our excitement was packed into a short space. The boys were on holiday, and all over the place. Mother was mostly in the kitchen, presiding over mincemeat and puddings. I was set to clean currants, squeeze lemons, and cut up candied peel.

Christmas Eve: A Suburban Scene

Barnholt lent a hand at chopping the suet, but kept making raids on the lumps of sugar tucked away in the candied peel, which he assured me were very hard and nasty in the mincemeat, but had no ill effects on him.

Tom and Dym kept going to Upper Street to get stationery, cards, and presents from the shops. Charles spent his time in painting home-made Christmas cards. Midday dinner was a noisy buzz of comparing notes on the morning's doings, and having a look at what Charles had produced. The afternoons were generally given up to the preparation of our annual play. It fell to Tom to devise the plot, and to Charles, the Bully Bottom of the family, fell nearly everything else. He took the part of the villain or the comic washerwoman, and kept thinking up ideas for improving the parts of the others. He taught me how to act when I wasn't speaking, how to listen with agitation, how to do 'by-play', how to swoon, and once even how to die. Dym was usually the hero, a bit stiff, but always dignified. Barnholt had to be given a part with little to say, because, however willing, he could not be relied on to remember the words, or improvise other ones. He would be a coachman or a footman, or perhaps only the scene-shifter. What he really loved was to be the policeman, coming in at the crisis with a "Ere, what's all this?', pulling out his note-book, wetting his thumb, and taking people's addresses. He knew his stuff for this perfectly, but it wouldn't always fit into melodrama.

Tom, to my great comfort, was prompter, and saved me from many a breakdown when I was swamped with nervousness. I didn't actually forget my words, but I should have done if Tom hadn't stood by smiling at me behind the screen.

Christmas Eve was the day we liked best. The morning was a frenzied rush for last rehearsals, last posting of cards, last buying of presents. My father came home early, laden with parcels. The tea-table was resplendent with bon-bons (crackers), sweets, and surprise cakes with icing on the top and threepenny-bits inside. The usual 'bread and butter first' rule was set aside, and we all ate and talked and laughed to our heart's content.

Then followed the solemn ascent to the study for the play. The boys had borrowed chairs from the bedrooms, and placed them in two rows: the front (stalls) for father, mother, and any aunt, uncle, or visitor who happened to be there, and the back (pit) for the servants, who attended with much gigglement.

Personally I was thankful when this nerve-strain was over, and we all crowded down into the breakfast-parlour. Here, earlier in the day, mother and I had arranged the presents – a little pile for each, and we all fell upon them with delight. We were never fussed up with a Christmas tree or stockings or make-believe about Santa Claus. Perhaps we were too hardheaded. Perhaps mother considered that waking up in the

Twelfth Night Party 1840s

small hours to look at stockings was a bad beginning for an exciting day. As it was, we had nice time before bed for peeping into our new books, and gloating over all the fresh treasures.

Christmas Day itself followed a regular ritual. Service at St Paul's was exactly the same as it is now, the same hymns and even the same decorations (knots of red velvet hung on the pillars). The post was the next excitement, and we displayed our cards on the mantelpiece. The traditional dinner of turkey and plum pudding and dessert was followed by a comatose afternoon, during which Barnholt cooked chestnuts incessantly on the bars of the grate, tossing them to us as they were done.

The evening festivities began with the ceremony of punch-making. This was always my father's special job, and he spread himself over it royally. Quantities of loaf sugar and lemons were assembled, and a very large glass jug. A kettle of water

was on the fire. The lemon-juice and sugar were stirred together at the bottom of the jug, then a tumblerful each of rum and brandy were added. Carefully my father then filled the jug with boiling water. Carefully, because once the boiling water smashed the jug, and everything splashed over the dining-room table. He laughed and called for all the ingredients over again. 'We've lost the punch,' said he, 'we needn't also lose a bit of our lives by crying over it.'

London Snow

ROBERT BRIDGES

Robert Bridges' poem London Snow *catches the mood of a city whose normal everyday sounds and frenzied activity are deadened by falling snow. Bridges, who was poet laureate from 1913 until his death in 1930, also trained to be a doctor and held various hospital appointments in London until 1882 when ill health made him retire to the country.*

When men were all asleep the snow came flying,
In large white flakes falling on the city brown,
Stealthily and perpetually settling and loosely lying,
    Hushing the latest traffic of the drowsy town;

Deadening, muffling, stifling its murmurs failing;
Lazily and incessantly floating down and down:
    Silently sifting and veiling road, roof and railing;
Hiding difference, making unevenness even,
Into angles and crevices softly drifting and sailing.
    All night it fell, and when full inches seven
It lay in the depth of its uncompacted lightness,
The clouds blew off from a high and frosty heaven;
    And all woke earlier for the unaccustomed brightness
Of the winter dawning, the strange unheavenly glare:
The eye marvelled – marvelled at the dazzling whiteness;
    The ear hearkened to the stillness of the solemn air;
No sound of wheel rumbling nor of foot falling,
And the busy morning cries came thin and spare.
    Then boys I heard, as they went to school, calling,
They gathered up the crystal manna to freeze
Their tongues with tasting, their hands with snowballing;
    Or rioted in a drift, plunging up to the knees;
Or peering up from under the white-mossed wonder,
'O look at the trees!' they cried, 'O look at the trees!'
    With lessened load a few carts creak and blunder,
Following along the white deserted way,
A country company long dispersed asunder:
    When now already the sun, in pale display
Standing by Paul's high dome, spread forth below
His sparkling beams, and awoke the stir of the day.
    For now doors open, and war is waged with the snow;
And trains of sombre men, past tale of number,
    Tread long brown paths, as toward their toil they go:
But even for them awhile no cares encumber
Their minds diverted; the daily word is unspoken,
The daily thoughts of labour and sorrow slumber
At the sight of the beauty that greets them, for the charm
    they have broken.

The Coronation of William the Conqueror

On Christmas Day 1066 a remarkable scene took place at Westminster Abbey. It was a year after the consecration of the Abbey church, and a new king was about to supplant the old Saxon line, bringing with him new customs and a new language. William, the Norman Conqueror, specifically wanted his ceremony to take place on the birthday of the 'Prince of Peace', but peace is the last thing his coronation will be remembered for.

The coronation took place within the abbey walls among a mixed assembly of Normans and Englishmen and began with all the pomp and ceremony expected of a king's coronation. Then the new sovereign was shown to the people, who were asked whether they accepted him as their lawful king. The people's consent was asked first in the Saxon language by Ealdred, Archbishop of York, who was conducting the proceedings, and then by the French Bishop of Coutances who repeated the question in Norman French.

At this point the solemn occasion gave way to enthusiastic cheers of acceptance from the assembled audience. But unfortunately the Norman guard of soldiers, waiting outside for their King, mistook the sounds for cries of hostility and believed William was being slaughtered by the English. A frenzy seized them as they hurled their lighted torches on to the straw-covered buildings around them and proceeded to plunder the contents. Most of those inside the church hurried out to see what was happening and they too became embroiled in the fray.

The ceremony, nevertheless, continued with those few who remained inside able to witness the king being annointed and crowned King of England. To bring the event to a hasty conclusion the sacrament was omitted as the new crown, which William had had made especially, rather than wear the old Saxon diadem, was placed on his head.

So it was, on Christmas Day and in these stormy circumstances, that Westminster Abbey established its long tradition as England's ceremonial centre and coronation church.

Christmas London

GEORGE R. SIMS

Apart from writing poetry and plays, Sims left a valuable record of late nineteenth-century London in the form of a series of articles written on everyday life in the capital. Living London was published in 1901 as a fortnightly part-work, and the chapter on Christmas is typically sentimental in tone, showing to what extent Christmas had become a popular commercial event affecting every level of society.

· A London Christmas ·

In the busy streets the market is at its height. The grocers are so gay with good things that grown-up men and women stop in front of them as fascinated as were Hansel and Gretel by the witch's cottage made to eat. The sweetmeat shops are so cunningly set out that even the aged dyspeptic feels his loose change burning a hole in his pocket. The stationers' shops are packed from morning till night with men, women, and children who are purchasing pictorial Christmas greetings that will tax the capacity of his Majesty's post office almost to the point of the last straw.

'Post early,' the Postmaster cries beseechingly for weeks before the festival, and the great public obeys. From the twentieth of December it begins to crowd into the post offices with hands full of envelopes and arms full of parcels, and the post office assistants, male and female, seem to become machines. They sacrifice themselves nobly to a grand cause. The flower girl has cried aloud in her weariness that she 'hates the smell of the roses,' but the loyal army that serves under the banner of the Postmaster-General has not yet given us one weakling to cry aloud that he (or she) hates Christmas.

Presently the bustle and the tumult, the crowding and confusion, are over, the streets that all through Christmas Eve have been like fairs grow gradually darker as the flickering lights go down and the shutters go up.

Thousands of men and women who earn their living in London have crowded the railway termini, and gone to their friends in the far-away towns. Londoners themselves have always the home feeling strongly upon them on Christmas Eve. It is a night to spend with the wife and bairns in happy, eager anticipation of the morrow. So the theatres are mostly closed, the music-halls are half empty, and even the street market grows deserted towards ten o'clock. Midnight finds the great thoroughfares given up to the policemen and a few stragglers. The great home festival has commenced.

9

The Waits

All London is under its own roof-tree waiting for Santa Claus.

But long before Christmas Eve has melted into Christmas Day mighty London has had mighty deeds to accomplish, that there may be no hitch in the preparations for the Gargantuan feast.

The great railway carriers have been at their wits' ends to deliver the parcels, the packages, the hampers, the cases of gifts and good things that have been entrusted to them. On hundreds of hampers the word 'Perishable' stares the officials in the face. But trains are late owing to the increase of the goods and passenger traffic. And the 'perishable' hampers arrive in such vast quantities that horses and men have to be kept at work night and day in order to deliver them. Sometimes it happens – it cannot be helped – that the long-expected poultry or game from the country that was to have been the Christmas fare is delivered to the disappointed householder just as the family are sitting down to something else purchased in despair at the last moment.

· *A London Christmas* ·

The theatres are mostly closed on Christmas Eve, but do not imagine that they are deserted. In some of them the preparations for the gorgeous Christmas pantomime which is to delight the children, young and old, on Boxing Day are in full swing. It is the dress rehearsal.

We pass the public-houses which are still open, but which are not thronged as usual. Here and there we come upon men carefully carrying the goose that they have secured in the goose club, and others who are carrying home the hamper of spirits and wine that Boniface has presented them with in return for their weekly subscription. But there is little noise, and there is a marked absence of the old riotous excess. London at Christmas time today is a great improvement on the Christmas London of the past.

Time creeps on, and the quiet hours have come. Now and again the old tunes float out on the silence of the night. 'The Mistletoe Bough' is rendered more melancholy than even the composer intended it to be by a cornet with a cold. The waits have had their day, but still in some parts of London they wake the sleeper from his pleasant dreams, and call for a Christmas-box in the morning. And the carollers still remain with us to sing the old world words that bear us back to the days of the yule log, the masquers, the mummers, the squire, the stage coach, and the snow-clad earth of the Christmas of our forefathers.

* * *

It is Christmas morning. London does not rise so early as usual today, and it is well on towards ten o'clock before there is any considerable movement. Then people, who are going to spend the day with friends in the suburbs or at some little distance, begin to make their way to the railway stations. Here are youths and maidens hastening by themselves, here an aged man and woman making their way slowly, here are family

Christmas Train 1870s

parties, papa, mamma, and olive branches innumerable. Almost without exception each bears a brown-paper parcel. It is the Christmas gift, the little present that is usually taken to the hosts by the visitors – to uncle John, to aunt Mary, to the cousins, to grandmamma and grandpapa.

All the morning long the little stream of parcel bearers going out to spend the day with relatives and friends continues, but towards eleven it is joined by another crowd, a crowd that carries a church service instead of a paper parcel, a crowd that is spending Christmas in its own home. The church bells are ringing merrily. When they cease there is a noticeable thinning of the stream of pedestrians. The trains on the local lines have ceased running until after Divine service, and now there are only the travellers who are taking 'bus and tram and cab to their destinations. The private carriages, the hired broughams, will not start with the little family parties outward bound until later in the day.

Up till half-past one there are always people in the streets taking the Christmas walk which is to prepare the appetite for dinner, a lengthy meal that taxes the digestive powers of most of us, and the parks and open spaces are fairly filled if the weather is fine. But after half-past one quiet reigns once more. London is indoors again. The richer folk are at lunch – the poorer folk are at dinner.

This is the hour to walk abroad observently and take an unobtrusive peep at the windows as you pass. Everywhere you see that it is Christmas Day. At many a window you can see the little ones happy with the gifts that Santa Claus has brought them. Little boys are already testing the strength of their playthings. Little girls are enjoying the first sweets of motherhood in their tender attentions to the new doll. The studious children and the romantic children are absorbed in the pages of the new story books.

Over the children's heads at the windows you have a glimpse of the table spread and waiting for the feast that is being dished up in the regions below. The fire light flickers and dances on the walls, and catches the bunch of holly over the mantelpiece and the evergreens twined in the gasalier. And up through the area railings there comes a fragrant odour that makes you look at your watch and remember your own luncheon hour.

From one to half-past there is a little stream of visitors to the workhouses and certain charitable institutions, where Christmas is being celebrated by a dinner to the inmates. Fashionable philanthropy which has contributed to the good cheer passes a pleasant half-hour on Christmas Day in assisting the poor, the lonely, and the afflicted to share in the common

· *A London Christmas* ·

'The Young Man who is alone on Christmas Day', from the
Illustrated London News, 21 December 1850

joy. Even in the great palaces of pain, where suffering is ever present and death rarely absent, the doctors, the nurses, and the students do their best to bring a little of the world's happiness to the bedside of the patient. For the children there are toys and Christmas trees, for the grown-up folk such fare and amusement as they can appreciate.

There are people, of course, who have nothing on Christmas Day, but they are few. Some by nature of their work have to make shift and take their Christmas dinner where they can. The 'bus driver may have to take his in the 'bus, but in his way he manages to make up a little family party. His wife brings the meat and the pudding in two basins, and she and his little daughter sit with him in the 'bus, and make it homelike. The conductor who is unmarried is invited to take a seat at the 'table.' Appreciating the kindly thought he goes into the public-house, fetches the beer, and pays for it.

The crossing-sweeper goes off duty after the folk have returned from church, and does not come on again till evening. He generally has a 'home,' and his table, if it does not actually 'groan,' is well covered with good things. For the charitable ladies of the neighbourhood have always a corner in their hearts for the crossing-sweeper, and many are the gifts he gets in the shape of creature comforts for his Christmas entertainment.

About four o'clock the Christmas dinners of the well-to-do begin. Except among the aristocracy it is a usual thing to make the dinner hour afternoon instead of evening. From four to seven you may picture family parties in almost every house you pass in the best neighbourhoods. The lamps of the street are just lighted, and darkness is setting in.

The blinds of the houses are drawn, but behind them you know that a united family are gathered round the board, and that merriment is the dominant note. From seven o'clock the sounds of festival strike your ears. You can hear the bang of the Christmas cracker, the merry laughter of the children, at times the sounds of an unmistakable romp. All over London the same spirit is present. Young and old have given themselves up to the joy of living.

from

The Diaries of Samuel Pepys

For Pepys, who lived in London all his life, the Christmas season would have been an extremely sociable and festive one. The diaries reveal that Christmas Day itself was usually fairly quiet. He would go to church and then spend the rest of the day with his wife and one or two other members of the family or close friends. On Boxing Day he'd take his 'boxes' to various tradesmen but apart from that there was little present-giving, though he once gave a New Year's gift to his mistress, Doll Lane, and in the New Year of 1669 he gave his wife an expensive walnut cabinet. This great naval administrator kept a diary only during the 1660s, after which his sight gave way.

Christmas Day, 1661. In the morning to church; where at the door of our pew I was fain to stay, because that the Sexton had not opened the door. A good sermon of Mr Mills. Dined at home all alone. And taking occasion, from some fault in the meat, to complain of my maid's Sluttery, my wife and I fell out, and I up to my Chamber in a discontent. After dinner my wife comes up to me and all friends again; and she and I to walk upon the Leads; and there Sir W. Pen called us and we

Christmas Dinner *c.* 1660

went to his house and supped with him. But before supper, Captain Cock came to us half-drunck and begun to talk; but Sir W. Pen, knowing his humour and that there was no end of his talking, drinks four great glasses of wine to him one after another, healths to the King &c., and by that means made him drunk, and so he went away; and so we sat down to supper and were merry; and so after supper home and to bed.

Christmas Day, 1663. Lay long, talking pleasantly with my wife; but among other things, she begin, I know not whether by design or chance, to enquire what she should do if I should by an accident die; to which I did give her some slight answer,

17

but shall make good use of it to bring myself to some settlement for her sake, by making a Will as soon as I can.

Up, and to church, where Mr Mills made an ordinary sermon; and so home and dined with great pleasure with my wife; and all the afternoon, first looking out at window and seeing the boys playing at many several sports in our back-yard by Sir W. Pens, which minded me of my own former times; and then I begin to read to my wife upon the globes, with great pleasure and to good purpose, for it will be pleasant to her and to me to have her understand those things.

In the evening to the office, where I stayed late reading Rushworth, which is a most excellent collection of the beginning of the late quarrels in this kingdom. And so home to supper and to bed with good content of mind.

Christmas Day, 1664. Up (my wife's eye being ill still of the blow I did in a passion give her on Monday last) to church alone – where Mr Mills, a good sermon. To dinner at home, where very pleasant with my wife and family. After dinner, I to Sir W. Batten's and there received so much good usage (as I have of late done) from him and my Lady, obliging me and my wife, according to promise, to come and dine with them tomorrow with our neighbours, that I was in pain all the day, and night too after, to know how to order the business of my wife's not going – and by discourse receive fresh instances of Sir J. Minnes's folly in complaining to Sir G. Carteret of Sir W. Batten and me for some family offences; such as my having of a stopcock to keep the water from them – which vexes me, but it would more, but that Sir G. Carteret knows him very well. Thence to the French church; but coming too late, I returned and to Mr Rawlinson's church, where I heard a good sermon of one that I remember was at Pauls with me, his name Maggett. And very great store of fine women there is in this church, more then I know anywhere else about us.

So home and to my chamber, looking over and setting in order my papers and books; and so to supper, and then to prayers and to bed.

Christmas Day, 1666. Lay pretty long in bed. And then rise, leaving my wife desirous to sleep, having sat up till 4 this morning seeing her maids make mince-pies. I to church, where our parson Mills made a good sermon. Then home, and dined well on some good ribs of beef roasted and mince pies; only my wife, brother, and Barker, and plenty of good wine of my own; and my heart full of true joy and thanks to God Almighty for the goodness of my condition at this day. After dinner I begun to teach my wife and Barker my song, *It is decreed* – which pleases me mightily, as now I have Mr Hinxton's bass. Then out, and walked alone on foot to Temple, it being a fine frost, thinking to have seen a play all alone; but there missing of any Bills, concluded there was none; and so back home, and there with my brother, reducing the names of all my books to an Alphabet, which kept us till 7 or 8 at night; and then to supper, W. Hewer with us, and pretty merry; and then to my chamber to enter this day's journal only, and then to bed – my head a little thoughtful how [to] behave myself in the business of the victualling, which I think will be prudence to offer my service in doing something in passing the purser's accounts – thereby to serve the King – get honour to myself, and confirm me in my place in the victualling, which at present hath not work enough to deserve my wages.

Christmas Eve, 1667. Up, and all the morning at the office; and at noon with my clerks to dinner and then to the office again, busy at the office till 6 at night; and then by coach to St James's, it being now about 6 at night, my design being to see the Ceremonys, this night being the Eve of Christmas, at the Queen's Chapel. But it being not begun, I to Westminster hall

and there stayed and walked; and then to the Swan and there
drank and talked, and did besar a little Frank; and so to
White-hall and sent my coach round, and I through the park
to chapel, where I got in up almost to the rail and with a great
deal of patience, stayed from 9 at night to 2 in the morning in
a very great Crowd; and there expected, but found nothing
extraordinary, there being nothing but a high Masse. The
Queen was there and some ladies. But Lord, what an odde
thing it was for me to be in a crowd of people, here a footman,
there a beggar, here a fine lady, there a zealous poor papist,
and here a Protestant, two or three together, come to see the
show. I was afeared of my pocket being picked very much. But
here I did make myself to do la cosa by mere imagination,
mirando a jolie mosa and with my eyes open, which I never did
before – and God forgive me for it, it being in the chapel.
Their music very good indeed, but their service I confess too
frivolous, that there can be no zeal go along with it; and I do
find by them themselfs, that they do run over their beads with
one hand, and point and play and talk and make signs with the
other, in the midst of their Masse. But all things very rich and
beautiful. And I see the papists had the wit, most of them, to
bring cushions to kneel on; which I wanted, and was mightily
troubled to kneel. All being done, and I sorry for my coming,
missing of what I expected; which was to have had a child
borne and dressed there and a great deal of do, but we broke up
and nothing like it done; and there I left people receiving the
sacrament, and the Queen gone, and ladies; only my [Lady]
Castlemayne, who looks prettily in her night-clothes. And so
took my coach, which waited, and away through Covent-
garden to set down two gentlemen and a lady, who came
thither to see also and did make mighty mirth in their talk of
the folly of this religion; and so I stopped, having set them
down, and drank some burnt wine at the Rose tavern door,
while the constables came and two or three Bell-men went by,

it being a fine light [25th] moonshine morning; and so home round the City and stopped and dropped money at five or six places, which I was the willinger to do, it being Christmas-day; and so home and there find wife in bed, and Jane and the maids making pyes, and so I to bed and slept well; and rose about 9, and to church and there heard a dull sermon of Mr Mills, but a great many fine people at church, and so home; wife and girl and I alone at dinner, a good Christmas dinner; and all the afternoon at home, my wife reading to me the history of the Drummer, of Mr Monpesson, which is a strange story of spirits, and worth reading indeed. In the evening comes Mr Pelling, and he sat and supped with us; and very good company, he reciting to us many copies of good verses of Dr Wilde, who writ *Iter Boreale*; and so to bed – my boy being gone with W. Hewer and Mr Hater to Mr Gibsons in the country to dinner, and lie there all night.

Seasonal Excesses

Holding fat stock shows and dressing butchers' windows with carcases during the Christmas season was thought by many to be a distasteful and brutal custom, as this article in Punch *of 1850 shows. Some shop owners covered every square inch of their premises with rank upon rank of joints and slaughtered game. Flocks of geese and turkeys from East Anglia were driven into the city and huge quantities*

· *A London Christmas* ·

*of freshly slaughtered animals came in on the Norfolk
coaches, each looking like a travelling butcher's shop.*

Nearly all the streets of London last week were more or less hung
with prize beef. Tallow chandlers and soap boilers, as they
looked upon the carcases, paid homage to the fat, and cooks and
kitchen maids dropped curtsies to perquisites in perspective.
But of all the show-beef exhibited, no carcase so worthily
appealed to the admiration of a discriminating public as the
carcase of an ox, destined, as we heard, for the Lord Mayor's
table during the dinner festivities of the season – it was no other
than the carcase of the bullock that, driven from Smithfield
Market, broke shop windows, knocked down horses, and in
Bowling-Green lane lifted an old woman 'into the air several
feet, letting her fall near the walls' of an appropriate burial

Newgate Market, on Christmas Eve

ground, which, as a final tenant, she narrowly escaped. Further, the bullock gored a man named Thomas Lagan, who two days afterwards died in St Bartholomews.

It will be readily conceded that this bullock was – especially for the City of London – the prize bullock of the season, as vindicating the civic wisdom that clings to Smithfield Market as a no less vital than venerable institution.

from

A Christmas Carol

CHARLES DICKENS

In 1843 A Christmas Carol *became a symbol throughout the English-speaking world of the new spirit of Christmas with its sudden transformation from merriment and conviviality to a preoccupation with good will and benevolence. Dickens conceived the idea for the story during long walks through the London streets – 'fifteen and twenty miles many a night when all the sober folks had gone to bed.' The book was a huge and instantaneous commercial success touching the conscience of the Victorian middle classes. It is no coincidence that in the year* A Christmas Carol *first appeared* Punch *asked its readers: 'What have you done, this "merry Christmas", for the*

happiness of those about, below you? Nothing? Do you dare, with those sirloin cheeks and that port-wine nose, to answer – Nothing?'

The first extract included here is a description of London street life on Christmas Eve. It also shows how short a London Christmas was in those days since Scrooge's clerk – Bob Cratchit – had no statutory rights to a day off on Boxing Day. The second extract describes Bob Cratchit's Christmas dinner with the entire family taking part in extensive preparations for their most memorable and extravagant meal of the year.

Meanwhile the fog and darkness thickened so, that people ran about with flaring links, proffering their services to go before horses in carriages, and conduct them on their way. The ancient tower of a church, whose gruff old bell was always peeping slily down at Scrooge out of a gothic window in the wall, became invisible, and struck the hours and quarters in the clouds, with tremulous vibrations afterwards as if its teeth were chattering in its frozen head up there. The cold became intense. In the main street at the corner of the court, some labourers were repairing the gas-pipes, and had lighted a great fire in a brazier, round which a party of ragged men and boys were gathered: warming their hands and winking their eyes before the blaze in rapture. The water-plug being left in solitude, its overflowings sullenly congealed, and turned to misanthropic ice. The brightness of the shops where holly sprigs and berries crackled in the lamp heat of the windows, made pale faces ruddy as they passed. Poulterers' and grocers' trades became a splendid joke: a glorious pageant, with which it was next to impossible to believe that such dull principles as bargain and sale had anything to do. The Lord Mayor, in the stronghold of the mighty Mansion House, gave orders to his fifty cooks and butlers to keep Christmas as a Lord Mayor's

Scrooge's Third Visitor: illustration by John Leech

household should; and even the little tailor, whom he had fined five shillings on the previous Monday for being drunk and bloodthirsty in the streets, stirred up tomorrow's pudding in his garret, while his lean wife and the baby sallied out to buy the beef.

Foggier yet, and colder! Piercing, searching, biting cold. If the good Saint Dunstan had but nipped the Evil Spirit's nose with a touch of such weather as that, instead of using his familiar weapons, then indeed he would have roared to lusty purpose. The owner of one scant young nose, gnawed and mumbled by the hungry cold as bones are gnawed by dogs, stooped down at Scrooge's keyhole to regale him with a Christmas carol: but at the first sound of

'God bless you, merry gentleman!
May nothing you dismay!'

Scrooge seized the ruler with such energy of action, that the singer fled in terror, leaving the keyhole to the fog and even more congenial frost.

At length the hour of shutting up the counting-house arrived. With an ill-will Scrooge dismounted from his stool, and tacitly admitted the fact to the expectant clerk in the Tank, who instantly snuffed his candle out, and put on his hat.

'You'll want all day tomorrow, I suppose?' said Scrooge.

'If quite convenient, Sir.'

'It's not convenient,' said Scrooge, 'and it's not fair. If I was to stop half-a-crown for it, you'd think yourself ill-used, I'll be bound?'

The clerk smiled faintly.

'And yet,' said Scrooge, 'you don't think *me* ill-used, when I pay a day's wages for no work.'

The clerk observed that it was only once a year.

'A poor excuse for picking a man's pocket every twenty-fifth of December!' said Scrooge, buttoning his great-coat to the chin. 'But I suppose you must have the whole day. Be here all the earlier next morning!'

The clerk promised that he would; and Scrooge walked out with a growl. The office was closed in a twinkling, and the clerk, with the long ends of his white comforter dangling

below his waist (for he boasted no great-coat), went down a slide on Cornhill, at the end of a lane of boys, twenty times, in honour of its being Christmas Eve, and then ran home to Camden Town as hard as he could pelt, to play at blindman's-buff.

Scrooge took his melancholy dinner in his usual melancholy tavern; and having read all the newspapers, and beguiled the rest of the evening with his banker's-book, went home to bed. He lived in chambers which had once belonged to his deceased partner. They were a gloomy suite of rooms, in a lowering pile of building up a yard, where it had so little business to be, that one could scarcely help fancying it must have run there when it was a young house, playing at hide-and-seek with other houses, and have forgotten the way out again. It was old enough now, and dreary enough, for nobody lived in it but Scrooge, the other rooms being all let out as offices. The yard was so dark that even Scrooge, who knew its every stone, was fain to grope with his hands. The fog and frost so hung about the black old gateway of the house, that it seemed as if the Genius of the Weather sat in mournful meditation on the threshold.

* * *

Such a bustle ensued that you might have thought a goose the rarest of all birds; a feathered phenomenon, to which a black swan was a matter of course – and in truth it was something very like it in that house. Mrs Cratchit made the gravy (ready beforehand in a little saucepan) hissing hot; Master Peter mashed the potatoes with incredible vigour; Miss Belinda sweetened up the apple-sauce; Martha dusted the hot plates; Bob took Tiny Tim beside him in a tiny corner at the table; the two young Cratchits set chairs for everybody, not forgetting themselves, and mounting guard upon their posts,

Christmas Pudding 1840s

crammed spoons into their mouths, lest they should shriek for goose before their turn came to be helped. At last the dishes were set on, and grace was said. It was succeeded by a breathless pause, as Mrs Cratchit, looking slowly all along the carving-knife, prepared to plunge it in the breast; but when she did, and when the long expected gush of stuffing issued forth, one murmur of delight arose all round the board, and even Tiny Tim, excited by the two young Cratchits, beat on the table with the handle of his knife, and feebly cried Hurrah!

There never was such a goose. Bob said he didn't believe there ever was such a goose cooked. Its tenderness and flavour, size and cheapness, were the themes of universal admiration. Eked out by the apple sauce and mashed potatoes, it was a sufficient dinner for the whole family; indeed, as Mrs Cratchit said with great delight (surveying one small atom of a bone upon the dish), they hadn't ate it all at last! Yet every one had had enough, and the youngest Cratchits in particular, were steeped in sage and onion to the eyebrows! But now, the plates being changed by Miss Belinda, Mrs Cratchit left the room alone – too nervous to bear witnesses – to take the pudding up and bring it in.

Suppose it should not be done enough! Suppose it should break in turning out! Suppose somebody should have got over the wall of the back-yard, and stolen it, while they were merry with the goose – a supposition at which the two young Cratchits became livid! All sorts of horrors were supposed.

Hallo! A great deal of steam! The pudding was out of the copper. A smell like a washing-day! That was the cloth. A smell like an eating-house and a pastrycook's next door to each other, with a laundress's next door to that! That was the pudding! In half a minute Mrs Cratchit entered – flushed, but smiling proudly – with the pudding, like a speckled cannon-ball, so hard and firm, blazing in half of half-a-quartern of ignited brandy, and bedight with Christmas holly stuck into the top.

Oh, a wonderful pudding! Bob Cratchit said, and calmly too, that he regarded it as the greatest success achieved by Mrs Cratchit since their marriage. Mrs Cratchit said that now the weight was off her mind, she would confess she had had her doubts about the quantity of flour. Everybody had something to say about it, but nobody said or thought it was at all a small pudding for a large family. It would have been flat heresy to do so. Any Cratchit would have blushed to hint at such a thing.

At last the dinner was all done, the cloth was cleared, the hearth swept, and the fire made up. The compound in the jug being tasted, and considered perfect, apples and oranges were put upon the table, and a shovel-full of chestnuts on the fire. Then all the Cratchit family drew round the hearth, in what Bob Cratchit called a circle, meaning half a one; and at Bob Cratchit's elbow stood the family display of glass. Two tumblers, and a custard-cup without a handle.

These held the hot stuff from the jug, however, as well as

golden goblets would have done; and Bob served it out with beaming looks, while the chestnuts on the fire sputtered and cracked noisily. Then Bob proposed:

'A Merry Christmas to us all, my dears. God bless us.'

Which all the family re-echoed.

'God bless us every one!' said Tiny Tim, the last of all.

from

The Paston Letters

Although Margaret Paston wrote this letter from Norfolk in 1443, it is addressed to her husband, John Paston, who spent at least half the year at his London chambers in the Temple defending their country estates from jealous rivals. Unlike today, there was no question of him interrupting London business to return home for a family Christmas, as the letter makes clear from its omission of any reference to seasonal activities. His wife, on the other hand, believed his poor health to be a good enough reason for his home-coming.

To my right worshipful husband, John Paston, dwelling in the Inner Temple at London, in haste.

Right worshipful husband, I recommend me to you, desiring

30

heartily to hear of your welfare, thanking God of your amending of the great disease that ye have had, and I thank you for the letter that ye sent me, for by my troth my mother and I were nought in heart's ease from the time that we wist of your sickness, till we wist verily of your amending.

My mother behested another image of wax of the weight of you, to our Lady of Walsingham, and she sent four nobles to the four Orders of friars at Norwich to pray for you, and I have behested to go on pilgrimage to Walsingham and to St Leonard's for you; by my troth I had never so heavy a season as I had from the time that I wist of your sickness, till I wist of your amending, and yet my heart is in no great ease, nor nought shall be, till I weet that ye be very whole.

I pray you heartily that ye will vouchsafe to send me a letter as hastily as ye may, if writing be none disease to you, and that ye will vouchsafe to send me word how your sore do. I would ye were at home, if it were your ease, and your sore might be looked to here as it is there ye be now, lever than a new gown though it were of scarlet. I pray you if your sore be whole, and so that ye may endure to ride when my father come to London, that ye will ask leave and come home when the horse should be sent home again, for I hope ye shall be kept as tenderly here as ye be at London. I may none leisure have to do write half a quarter so much as I should say to you if I might speak with you. I shall send you another letter as hastily as I may. I thank you that ye would vouchsafe to remember my girdle, and that ye would write to me at the time, for I suppose that writing was none ease to you. Almighty God have you in his keeping, and send you health. Written at Oxnead, in right great haste.

Yours, M. PASTON.

Christmas, 1443.

My mother greet you well, and sendeth you God's blessing and hers; and she prayeth you, and I pray you also, that ye be well

dieted of meat and drink, for that is the greatest help that ye may have now to your healthward. Your son fareth well, blessed be God.

from

The Siege of London

ROBERT HENREY

Published in 1946 this little-known book is an account of London during the Blitz. Although rationing meant that Christmas was no longer a time of excess and extravagance, Londoners still retained some vestige of the spirit of Christmas despite the terrible devastation done to the capital. The following extracts describe events that took place in London during the Christmas of 1942. The first extract refers to when a V2 dropped on a pub in Duke Street, skirting the eastern wing of Selfridges, and the second extract describes a Christmas Day service at Westminster Abbey attended by both soliders and civilians.

· A London Christmas ·

In Covent Garden Market

Some pages back I claimed that so far there was no outward sign of Christmas, but I had not visited Selfridge's, in which case I would undoubtedly have been able to write about the fir-trees illuminated with coloured globes and decorated with gay parcels which stood in every window along the whole length of the building from Orchard Street to Duke Street.

These must have made a very pleasant sight and charmed the shoppers who daily surge along this famous thoroughfare. But now these poor little trees, with the ornaments torn from them, lay amongst the broken glass on the pavement, and some of them were being swept into the gutter. Such a dismal picture would have needed the genius of Hans Andersen to commit it to paper, for what can be more pathetic than a garlanded tree that comes to a tragic end two and a half weeks before Christmas Day?

The excitement which this bomb caused was quite extraordinary. I think it was not entirely due to the fact that it was the first of its kind to fall in the West End – though that in itself was something. Probably there was a feeling of rage that after mastering its predecessor the V1, after pushing the Germans back to their frontiers, after dismissing the Home Guard and partially lifting the black-out, after hearing our politicians tell us that the bomb menace was virtually at an end, and after resigning ourselves to another Christmas at war, we should be plagued by these meteors which were now likely to increase rather than to diminish.

There was a trail of broken glass along Oxford Street, down Orchard Street, and halfway up Wigmore Street. The shopping crowds were not any smaller because of what the authorities call a major incident. Many women must have fallen upon it unawares, being less informed than we who lived within a quarter of a mile. The shop girls must have been surprised also, and as soon as they had clocked in, they were given brushes and pans to clean up the debris in the various departments, before the store was opened to the public.

But in this there was nothing new. We had seen it everywhere during the raids of 1940–1 and again during the February–March raids of this year, and during the devastating battle of the flying bombs. The chief difference was in the speed and mechanization of rescue and repair work which was going on swiftly and methodically behind the barriers. The American squads, organized and supplied on military lines, applied the large-scale American technique to the job.

· *A London Christmas* ·

Londoners could no longer wander amongst the wreckage as they could in the early days of the war. The public was kept to the outer perimeter, which was a good thing because, as it was, one saw women calmly wheeling their prams whilst the shopkeepers shovelled out glass from upper windows.

But while people were surging round the cordon, gaping at the strange tricks of blast and crowding into the shops, men of the heavy rescue squad were digging for bodies under the wreckage inside the cordon, and half a dozen members of the Women's Voluntary Service, wearing their green overcoats and berets, were by close and sympathetic interrogation disentangling the tragedies of the night at their post in the classroom of a girls' school, the windows of which were all broken.

They sat, these women, at a deal table against the wall at the far end of the room, and because it was bitterly cold, most of them had wrapped rugs round their knees. I drew up a chair and sat beside them, listening to the stories of all the poor folk who, with drawn faces and clothes grimed with dust and minute particles of plaster, had come to inquire about relatives or neighbours, injured, dead, or missing. . .

*   *   *

Christmas Day was white – not with snow, but with hoar-frost that lay like a crisp carpet over the parks. The temperature, below zero, contracted the muscles of one's face, and froze the puddles on the gravel walks. The sump, facing the Cornish elms in the Green Park Drawing-room, had a coating of ice, and the roofs of the black huts studded round the big searchlight looked as if somebody had decorated them with sugar-icing. A crimson sun, low in the sky in the direction of Victoria, was trying hard to penetrate the white mist that shrouded the wintry scene, and the searchlight, which was full on when I passed it, cast a bluish tint on the naked boughs of the maple-trees screening it from the deserted bandstand. Two soldiers were sawing logs behind the cookhouse door, and from the courtyard of Buckingham Palace came the strains of a military band playing an old-fashioned waltz.

There were few people about – half a dozen American soldiers and a woman exercising her poodle. The Mall was quite deserted, and on one of the railings of the suspension bridge which crosses the lake in St James's Park, I read these words written in the frost: 'Doris Regina Rogers – a happy Christmas.' Who was the girl with this regal name? Had she been out walking early with a soldier friend, who, while bending over the bridge very close to her, had written this message of love as he might have carved her initials on the trunk of beech or poplar? The towers of Westminster Abbey, shrouded in mist, took on their medieval aspect, powerful and mysterious. Big Ben tolled the hour, and a taxicab, its hood quite white, drew up at the abbey door, and I followed the occupants inside, where a tall fir-tree, decorated with coloured electric globes, stood in front of the tomb of the Unknown Warrior, at the four corners of which burned immense yellow candles whose flames, bent by the draught, caused the wax to drip. The scene of the nativity against a coloured oriental backcloth, was softly lit. The nave was warm and wrapped in meditation, and from afar came the voice of the preacher, himself invisible until one had passed silently along the aisle past the organ bridge.

Then one saw him in his white surplice and black stole with a touch of crimson, venerably dignified and austere against the ebony screen carved in front of the massive, fluted, and half-dim pillar of Normandy stone. All the candles of the high altar were glimmering and flickering, shedding a soft yellow and diffused light on fir-trees, tapestry, and gold plate. The canon in residence, his head bowed, was seated to the left of the communion table, and nearer to the pulpit sat two vergers who by and by would escort the preacher back to his place in the choir stalls. But just now his voice rose and fell melodiously, whilst the vast congregation was so hidden in shadow that one felt rather than perceived its presence.

But the abbey was less filled with khaki than I had expected it to be, and yet – I should have guessed that this would be so, for were not nearly all our troops of this theatre of war in Belgium and Holland, whilst the Americans were, at this very moment, engaged in the most bitter fighting since the invasion of the Continent?

For more than a week our thoughts had never left them. Anxiety had gripped us this Christmas, and Rundstedt's sudden and vicious attack had brought misery back to the liberated countries, threatening Liège, Sedan – even Brussels and Paris. Mentally we had reeled under the blow, and the holiday spirit had been singularly damped. We had thought more of the weather than of shopping. Had it not been for the children, we should have dispensed with holly, mistletoe, and pantomines. The fog had hung dismally over London as it enshrouded the battle area. We had welcomed two bright days with a sudden lifting of our spirits, and never had we greater cause to drop on our knees this Christmas morning to seek communion with our Maker.

Christmas Box

The old Christmas custom of the Christmas box was a way of giving gifts to servants and others who gave services throughout the year. Servants would ask their masters and their master's customers, such as brewers, bakers and cooks, for Christmas donations and often incur much ill feeling as a result. In 1849 Punch *published a stinging attack on the Christmas box tradition.*

The Christmas box system is, in fact, a piece of horribly internecine strife between cooks and butcher's boys, lamplighters, beadles, and all classes of society tugging at each other's pockets for the sake of what can be got under the pretext of seasonable benevolence. Our cooks bully our butchers for the annual box, and our butchers take it out of us in the course of the year by tacking false tails on to our saddles of mutton, adding false feet to our legs of lamb, and chousing us with large lumps of chump in our chops, for the purpose of adding to the bills by giving undue weight to our viands.

The tradition of the Christmas box of course lives on today with people who have provided services throughout the year, such as dustmen and postmen; it often provokes the same kind of hostile reaction. In the past, few minded if the services were worthwhile, but all too often they were not.

A long and laboured poem would frequently accompany the request for an offering, as for instance this one from a newsman.

· *A London Christmas* ·

Hail Christmas, once more, with thy train
   Of mirth, seeking gay happy faces,
Few examples of trouble or pain,
   But thy presence would drive from their places.

When thy name e'en brings to the mind
   A many bright Christmas that's past,
Spent with relations and friends good and kind,
   Of such days may you ne'er see the last.

CHRISTMAS! – that sound hath the power to charm,
   No matter what age or condition,
E'en the *News-boy* will brighten and warm
   As again he presents his *Petition*.

And trusts that he may not intrude,
   Since sanctioned by ages long past,
Then deem him not forward or rude,
   For old customs ought always to last.

For old customs, old friends, and old times,
   Was always considered the best,
Not forgetting likewise good old wines,
   When old friends to old wines adds a zest.

And should your *News-boy* be allowed
   To again make his bow at your door,
It will make him feel happy and proud,
   That his faults are forgiven once more.

For to faults he must certainly own,
   Few from them are found quite exempt,
So, while then a few I set down,
   The excuses pray not treat with contempt.

· *A London Christmas* ·

It's a fault for to bring them too late –
  To bring them too soon is another;
'Tis wrong for to not shut the gate,
  Or one paper to leave for another.

To bring them dirty, or all over mud,
  Is decidedly wrong altogether;
Or the reading not plain – being rub'd,
  As will happen sometimes in wet weather.

In short, there might be a few more
  Of little existing abuses.
But before I go seeking for more,
  I'd best find for those some excuses.

What many things make papers late,
  Express from Holland, from France, or from Spain,
Or last night in the House late debate
  Or the engine has broke once again.

Or a 'Murder!' with Trial in Kent;
  Reporters sent down with all diligence:
The papers kept back, all intent,
  In giving the latest intelligence.

But a reason still greater than these –
  Allowing papers quite soon are all out,
All folded and sorted suppose,
  He starts on his long dreary rout.

But as there's a great distance to go,
  Neither heeding foul weather or fine,
But must needs begin early you know,
  That the last may be served in good time.

But alas! your *too soon*, so in vain
   Bolts and knockers become in requisition;
You may ring and knock – then ring again,
   All asleep, from the garret to kitchen;

And thinking, while waiting, how strange,
   As thoughts flow from one to the other,
Because he's too soon for the one,
   It will make him too late for another.

While hastening to fetch up lost time,
   So as not to let further friends wait,
For his thought are on them all the time,
   Hurry on, and so *not shut the gate*.

The papers, you must now understand,
   Are all of them laid in rotation,
As their turn comes, are took up by the hand,
   And each left to their own destination.

And, as houses might lay far and wide,
   With the mind of sometimes in a bother,
Took for once, perhaps, from the wrong side,
   And so might leave one for the other.

And, as papers are all of them damp,
   And damp things will, of course, cling together,
In taking out, one wicked scamp
   In the mud sure will tumble another.

So now my kind Patrons and Friends,
   Having not one more single excuse,
Your forgiveness I hope you'l extend,
   And your kindness I will never abuse.

But your smiles whether gain'd, cannot know,
  And my hopes be all cast on the rocks,
But a proof is still left — if you show
  Your forgiveness in a kind CHRISTMAS BOX!!

from

Christmas (1851) in the Metropolis

CHARLES MANBY SMITH

For the London citizen who required the custom of various tradesmen throughout the year, Boxing Day could be anything but a joy, as this amusing extract from an article by Charles Manby Smith shows. It appeared in Chamber's Journal, December 1852, *and refers to the custom of the Christmas box, seen by many to be a form of blackmail and begging rather than genuine remuneration for services rendered. This kind of door-to-door knocking would take place on Boxing Day, from where the name probably derived.*

We can hardly close these desultory sketches of Christmas-time without some brief allusion to the day after Christmas, which, through every nook and cranny of the great Babel, is known and recognised as 'Boxing Day,' – the day consecrated to *baksheesh*, when nobody, it would almost seem, is too proud to beg, and when everybody who does not beg is expected to play the almoner. 'Tie up the knocker – say you're sick, you are dead,' is the best advice perhaps that could be given in such cases to any man who has a street-door and a knocker upon it. Now is your time to make out a new list of occupations, and to become acquainted with all the benefactors whose good offices you have been enjoying all the year through without one thought of the gratitude you owe them. Dab the first is the sweep, of course, who must be paid over again for sweeping your chimneys. Half fearing that if you refuse you may get a smoky house for the rest of the year, you consent for the sake of your lungs, and he is off. You sit down to breakfast, and with

'The Man who gave Half a Crown Last Year'; Bateman Cartoon
1920

43

the first slice of toast comes dab the second. You glance out of the window, and see a couple of long-coated varlets bearing battered French horns, and you cheerfully bestow another shilling on the minstrels, as you suppose of the wet and dismal nights. They are off to the next door, and before you have drunk your second cup comes dab the third – the turncock wants *his* water-rate. You do as you like with him, but if you turn him off empty, he does the same with the water, and leaves you dependent on your neighbours for a supply. Dab the fourth is the dustman, and you must down with your dust, or you will get the dust down your throat the next time the bin has to be cleared out. Dab the fifth waters the roads in summer, and wants to wet his whistle at your expense. Dab the sixth scrapes them in winter, and now comes to scrape acquaintance with you in the affectionate desire of drinking your health 'at this jiful season.' Dab the seventh – what! the waits again? 'I gave the fellow a shilling just now.' 'Yes, sir,' says Betty, 'but them fellows had no right to it.' Here the leader and spokesman of the band of *genuine* waits makes his appearance, bowing and scraping at the parlour-door: 'Sorry to *hob*trude, sir, but ours is the genuine waits, sir. That there gang what you subscribed, sir, only goes a collectin' – they never plays nothin'; they aint musicians, only thievin' scamps as robs honest men. You rek'lect my vice, sir, a wishin' of you a merry Christmas and a happy new year.' Of course you recognise his 'vice,' for he bellows as loud as he did last Wednesday at midnight, and of course, too, you pay the shilling over again. Dab the eighth is the lamp-lighter, who enlightens you on the subject of his large merits and small pay. Dab the ninth is the grocer's boy, who is followed by a shoal of dabs in regular succession, comprising every mentionable trade, until at length your patience being exhausted, and your small-change at the same low ebb, you rush desperately into a greatcoat and out of the house, and leave Betty to fight the battle of *baksheesh* as well as she can, which she generally does victoriously by declining to show a front to the enemy, and leaving the dabs to come as slowly as they choose to the unwilling conviction, that 'it's no use knocking at the door any more.'

Frost Fairs on the Thames

Between the sixteenth and nineteenth centuries the Thames froze nine times and created a unique setting for midwinter entertainment. What was remarkable about the fairs was that fashionable society mingled happily with city low-life, as butchers, bakers, barbers, goldsmiths and weavers set up their tents on the frozen river. Law students from the Temple, 'always great patrons of revels and sports', were particularly partial to the fairs and the temptations of oysters, pancakes, plum cake, hot pudding pies and handmade chocolate. Winter sports like sledging and skating also took place, alongside skittles and bowls. Men gambled at lotteries, and boats fitted with wheels and decorated with flags and streamers were for hire.

The severe frost of 1715–16 was short but 'devastating' and several post-boys were actually frozen to death. *Dawk's Newsletter* of 14 January has a vivid description of that winter's frost:

The Thames seems now a solid rock of ice, and booths for the sale of brandy, wine, ale and other exhilarating liquors, have been for some time fixed there on; but now it is in a manner like a town: thousands of people cross it, and with wonder view the mountainous heaps of water, that now lie congealed into ice. On Thursday, a great cook's-shop was erected, and gentlemen went as frequently to dine there, as at any ordinary. Over against Westminster, Whitehall and Whitefriars, Printing-presses are kept upon the ice, where many persons have their names printed, to transmit the wonders of the season to posterity. Coaches, waggons, carts etc. were driven on it, and an enthusiastic preacher, held forth to a motley congregation on the mighty waters, with a zeal fiery enough to have thawed himself through the ice, had it been susceptible to religious warmth. This, with other pastimes and diversions, attracted the attention of many of the nobility, and brought the Prince of Wales to visit the Frost Fair.

This account also exists of when the Thames froze in 1739–40:

The winter of 1739–40, became memorable from its uncommon severity, and occurance of one of the most intense frosts that had ever been known in this country, and which from its piercing cold, and long continuance, has been recorded in our annals by the appellation of the GREAT FROST.

It commenced on Christmas-day, and lasted till the 17th of the following FEBRUARY, when it began to break up, but was not wholly dissipated till near the end of the month. The distress which it occasioned among the poor and labouring classes in London, was extreme: coals could hardly be obtained for money, and water was equally scarce.

The watermen and fishermen, with a peter-boat in

Frost Fair on the River Thames

mourning, and the carpenters, bricklayers, etc. with their tools and utensils in mourning, walked through the streets in large bodies, imploring relief for their own and families' necessities; and, to the honour of the British character, this was liberally bestowed. SUBSCRIPTIONS were also made in different parishes, and great benefactions bestowed by the opulent, through which the calamities of the season were much mitigated.

A few days after the frost had set in, great damage was done among the shipping in the River Thames by a high wind, which broke many vessels from their moorings, and drove them foul of each other, while the large flakes of ice there floated on the stream, overwhelming various boats and lights, and sunk several corn and coal vessels. By these accidents many lives were lost; and many others were also destroyed by the intenseness of the cold, both on land and water. Above bridge, the Thames was completely frozen over, and tents and numerous booths were erected on it for selling liquors, etc. to the multitudes that daily flocked thither for curiosity or diversion. The scene here displayed was very irregular, and had more the appearance of a fair on land, than of a frail exhibition, the only basis of which was congealed water. Various shops were opened for the sale of toys, cutlery, and other light articles, and all the common sports of the populace in a wintery season, were carried on with the augmented spirit, in despite or forgetfulness of the distress which reigned on show. Many of the houses which at that time stood upon London-Bridge, as well as the bridge itself, received considerable damage when the thaw commenced, by the driving of ice.

(From *Frostiana – or a A History of the River Thames of the River Thames in a frozen state. Printed and published on the Ice on the River Thames, February 5th, 1814, by G. Davis.*)

from

Diary of a Provincial Lady

E.M. DELAFIELD

E.M. Delafield became a household name in England between the wars, and her books crystalize the mentality

and morality of the English ruling class in the Edwardian and George the Fifth periods. It was when she moved to Devon after the First World War that she began to scribble down the domestic disasters and routine follies of this curiously dry-witted heroine, who like so many of her provincial counterparts came to London every year to do her Christmas shopping.

December 17th, London. Come up to dear Rose's flat for two days' Christmas shopping, after prolonged discussion with

Shopping in the Lowther Arcade

Sixties fashion show outside Selfridges

Robert, who maintains that All can equally well be done by Post.

Take early train so as to get in extra afternoon. Have with me Robert's old leather suit-case, own ditto in fibre, large quantity of chrysanthemums done up in brown paper for Rose, small packet of sandwiches, handbag, fur coat in case weather turns cold, book for journey, and illustrated paper kindly presented by Mademoiselle at the station. (Query suggests itself: Could not some of these things have been dispensed with, and if so which?)

Bestow belongings in the rack, and open illustrated paper with sensation of leisured opulence, derived from unwonted absence of all domestic duties . . .

December 19th. Find Christmas shopping very exhausting. Am paralysed in the Army and Navy Stores on discovering that List of Xmas Presents is lost, but eventually run it to earth in Children's Books Department. While there choose book for dear Robin, and wish for the hundredth time that Vicky had been less definite about wanting Toy Greenhouse and *nothing else*. This apparently unprocurable. (*Mem.*: Take early opportunity of looking up story of the Roc's Egg to tell Vicky.)

Rose says 'Try Selfridge's'. I protest, but eventually go there, find admirable – though expensive – Toy Greenhouse, and unpatriotically purchase it at once. Decide not to tell Robert this.

Choose appropriate offerings for Rose, Mademoiselle, William, and Angela – (who will be staying with us, so gifts must be above calendar-mark) – and lesser trifles for everyone else. Unable to decide between almost invisibly small diary, and really handsome card, for Cissie Crabbe, but eventually settle on diary, as it will fit into ordinary-sized envelope.

51

December 20th. Rose takes me to see St John Ervine's play, and am much amused. Overhear one lady in stalls ask another: Why don't *you* write a play, dear? Well, says the friend, it's so difficult, what with one thing and another, to find *time.* Am staggered. (Query: Could I write a play myself? Could we *all* write plays, if only we had the time? Reflect that St J.E. lives in the same county as myself, but feel that this does not constitute sound excuse for writing to ask him how he finds the time to write plays.)

December 22nd. Return home. One bulb in partial flower, but not satisfactory.

from

The Masque of Christmas

BEN JONSON

Written in 1616, this was apparently meant to be performed in the Curriers Hall but was transferred to the Court because the Curriers were too busy. It concerns a Londoner's Christmas and was written by Jonson for a London

audience. In the masque, Jonson introduces the main aspects of Christmas as the ten children of Mr Gregory Christmas (one of the earliest portraits of Father Christmas), naming them as Misrule, Carol, Minced-Pye, Gambol, Post and Pair (a popular card game), New Yeare's Gift, Mumming, Wassail, Offering and Baby Cake.

The masque as a form of drama was perfected in the reign of James I, and Jonson wrote a great many in collaboration with the architect Inigo Jones who designed the costumes and stage sets. But this kind of court entertainment more or less disappeared during the Civil War, along with the Royalists who had favoured it.

The Court being seated,
Enter CHRISTMAS, *with two or three of the Guard, attired in round Hose, long Stockings, a close Doublet, a high-crowded Hat, with a Brooch, a long thin Beard, a Truncheon, little Ruffes, white Shoos, his Scarfes and Garters tied cross, and his Drum beaten before him.*

WHY, Gentlemen, do you know what you doe? Ha! would you have kept me out? CHRISTMAS, old Christmas, Christmas of *London*, and Captayn Christmas? Pray you, let me be brought before my Ld. Chamberlayn, Ile not be answered else: *'Tis merry in hall, when beards wag all.*

The Truth is, I have brought a Masque here, out o' the Citty, of my own making, and do present it by a Sett of my Sons, that come out of the Lanes of *London*, good dancing Boyes all. It was intended, I confess, for *Curriers'-Hall*; but because the Weather has been open, and the Liverie were not at Leisure to see it till a Frost came, that they cannot worke, I thought it convenient, with some little Alterations, and the Groome o' the Revells hand to 't, to fit it for a higher Place; which I have done, and though I say it, another Manner of Device than your *New Yeares Night*. Bones o' bread, the King!

(*seeing his Mjty.*) Son *Rowland*! son *Clem*! be readie there in a Trice: quick boyes!

Enter his SONS and DAUGHTERS (ten in Number), led in, in a string, by CUPID, who is attired in a flat Capp, and a Prentice's Coat, with Winges at his Shoulders.

MISRULE, in a velvet Capp, with a sprigg, a short Cloke, great yellow Ruffe (like a Reveller); his Torche-bearer bearing a Rope, a Cheese, and a Baskett.

CAROL, a long tawny Coat, with a red Capp, and a Flute at his Girdle; his Torche-bearer carrying a Song-booke open.

MINCED-PYE, like a fine Cook's wife, drest neat; her Man carrying a Pye, Dish, and Spoones.

GAMBOL, like a Tumbler, with a Hoope and Bells; his Torche-bearer armed with a Colt-staff and a Binding-Cloth.

POST AND PAIR, with a Pair-royal of Aces in his Hat; his Garment all done over with Pairs and Purs; his 'Squire carrying a Boxe, Cards and Counters.

NEW YEARE'S GIFT, in a blue Coat, serving-man-like, with an Orange, and a sprigg of Rosemary gilt on his Head, his Hat full of Brooches, with a Collar of Gingerbread; his Torche-bearer carrying a March-Pane with a Bottle of Wine on either arme.

MUMMING, in a masquing pied Suit, with a Vizard; his Torche-bearer carrying the Boxe, and ringing it.

WASSEL, like a neat Sempster and Songster; her Page bearing a brown Bowle, drest with Ribbands, and Rosemary before her.

OFFERING, in a short Gowne, with a Porter's Staffe in his Hand, a Wyth borne before him, and a Bason, by his Torche-Bearer.

BABY-CAKE, drest like a Boy, in a fine long Coat, Biggin-bib, Muck-ender, and a little Dagger; his Usher bearing a great Cake, with a Beane and a Pease.

They enter singing.

Now God preserve, as you do well deserve,
   Your Majesties all two there;
Your Highnesse small, with my good Lords all,
   And Ladies, how do you do there?

Give me leave to ask, for I bring you a Masque
   From little, little, little London,
Which saye the King likes, I have passed the Pikes,
   If not, old Christmas is undone.

                [Noise without.]

Written on Christmas Day 1797

CHARLES LAMB

Christmas is not always a happy occasion. For some it can be a time for reflection and haunting memories of Christmas past. This poem by Lamb is about his sister, Mary, who had at the time been removed from the family home due to her madness.

· A London Christmas ·

*Lamb loved London with a passion. Born in Crown
Office Row in the Inner Temple, he once declared, 'I was
born, as you have heard, in a crowd. This has begot in me
an entire affection for that way of life, amounting to an
almost insurmountable aversion from solitude and rural
scenes.'*

I am a widow'd thing, now thou art gone;
Now thou art gone, my own familiar friend,
Companion, sister, help-mate, counsellor!
Alas! that honour'd mind, whose sweet reproof
And meekest wisdom in times past have smooth'd
The unfilial harshness of my foolish speech,
And made me loving to my parents old,
(Why is this so, ah, God! why is this so?)
That honour'd mind become a fearful blank,
Her senses lock'd up, and herself kept out
From human sight or converse, while so many
Of the foolish sort are left to roam at large,
Doing all acts of folly, and sin, and shame?
Thy paths are mystery!
        Yet I will not think,
Sweet friend, but we shall one day meet, and live
In quietness, and die so fearing God.
Or if *not*, and these false suggestions be
A fit of the weak nature, loth to part
With what it loved so long, and held so dear;
If thou art to be taken, and I left
(More sinning, yet unpunish'd save in thee),
It is the will of God, and we are clay
In the potter's hands; and, at the worst, are made
From absolute nothing, vessels of disgrace,
Till, his most righteous purpose wrought in us,
Our purified spirits find their perfect rest.

from

The Diary of a Nobody

GEORGE AND WEEDON GROSSMITH

The Victorian lower middle class Christmas is perhaps best summed up in The Diary of a Nobody *with Mr Pooter's account of life in the then highly respectable neighbourhood of Holloway. The book, which was first serialized in* Punch *in the 1890s, has become a classic of English humour, celebrating the Victorian bourgeoisie through this minor City clerk's transparent self-importance and suburban smugness.*

December 20. Went to Smirksons', the drapers, in the Strand, who this year have turned out everything in the shop and devoted the whole place to the sale of Christmas cards. Shop crowded with people, who seemed to take up the cards rather roughly, and, after a hurried glance at them, throw them down again. I remarked to one of the young persons serving, that carelessness appeared to be a disease with some purchasers. The observation was scarcely out of my mouth, when my thick coat-sleeve caught against a large pile of expensive cards in boxes one on top of the other, and threw them down. The manager came forward, looking very much annoyed, and picking up several cards from the ground, said to one of the assistants, with a palpable side-glance at me: 'Put these amongst the sixpenny goods; they can't be sold for a shilling now.' The result was, I felt it my duty to buy some of these damaged cards.

I had to buy more and pay more than intended. Unfortunately I did not examine them all, and when I got home I discovered a vulgar card with a picture of a fat nurse with two babies, one black and the other white, and the words: 'We wish Pa a Merry Christmas.' I tore up the card and threw it away. Carrie said the great disadvantage of going out in Society and increasing the number of our friends was, that we should have to send out nearly two dozen cards this year.

December 21. To save the postman a miserable Christmas, we follow the example of all unselfish people, and send out our cards early. Most of the cards had finger-marks, which I did not notice at night. I shall buy all future cards in the daytime. Lupin (who, ever since he has had the appointment with a stock and share broker, does not seem overscrupulous in his dealings) told me never to rub out the pencilled price on the backs of the cards. I asked him why. Lupin said: 'Suppose your card is marked 9d. Well, all you have to do is to pencil a 3 – and a long down-stroke after it – in *front* of the ninepence, and people will think you have given five times the price for it.'

In the evening Lupin was very low-spirited, and I reminded him that behind the clouds the sun was shining. He said: 'Ugh! it never shines on me.' I said: 'Stop, Lupin, my boy; you are worried about Daisy Mutlar. Don't think of her any more. You ought to congratulate yourself on having got off a very bad bargain. Her notions are far too grand for our simple tastes.' He jumped up and said: 'I won't allow one word to be uttered against her. She's worth the whole bunch of your

Christmas in an omnibus

friends put together, that inflated sloping-head of a Perkupp
included.' I left the room with silent dignity but caught my
foot in the mat.

December 23. I exchanged no words with Lupin in the morning;
but as he seemed to be in exuberant spirits in the evening I
ventured to ask him where he intended to spend his Christmas. He replied: 'Oh, most likely at the Mutlars'.'

In wonderment, I said: 'What! after your engagement has
been broken off?'

Lupin said: 'Who said it is off?'

I said: 'You have given us both to understand – '

He interrupted me by saying: 'Well, never mind what I said. *It is on again – there!*'

December 24. I am a poor man, but I would gladly give ten shillings to find out who sent me the insulting Christmas card I received this morning. I never insult people; why should they insult me? The worst part of the transaction is, that I find myself suspecting all my friends. The handwriting on the envelope is evidently disguised, being written sloping the wrong way. I cannot think either Gowing or Cummings would do such a mean thing. Lupin denied all knowledge of it, and I believe him; although I disapprove of his laughing and sympathizing with the offender. Mr Franching would be above such an act; and I don't think any of the Mutlars would descend to such a course. I wonder if Pitt, that impudent clerk at the office, did it? Or Mrs Birrell, the charwoman, or Burwin-Fosselton? The writing is too good for the former.

Christmas Day. We caught the 10.20 train at Paddington, and spent a pleasant day at Carrie's mother's. The country was quite nice and pleasant, although the roads were sloppy. We dined in the middle of the day, just ten of us, and talked over old times. If everybody had a nice, *un*interfering mother-in-law, such as I have, what a deal of happiness there would be in the world. Being all in good spirits, I proposed her health; and I made, I think, a very good speech.

I concluded, rather neatly, by saying: 'On an occasion like this – whether relatives, friends, or acquaintances – we are all inspired with good feelings towards each other. We are of one mind, and think only of love and friendship. Those who have quarrelled with absent friends should kiss and make up. Those who happily have *not* fallen out, can kiss all the same.'

I saw the tears in the eyes of both Carrie and her mother, and must say I felt very flattered by the compliment. That dear old Reverend John Panzy Smith, who married us, made a most cheerful and amusing speech, and said he should act on my suggestion respecting the kissing. He then walked round the table and kissed all the ladies, including Carrie. Of course one did not object to this: but I was more than staggered when a young fellow named Moss, who was a stranger to me, and who had scarcely spoken a word through dinner, jumped up suddenly with a sprig of mistletoe, and exclaimed: 'Hulloh! I don't see why I shouldn't be in on this scene.' Before one could realize what he was about to do, he kissed Carrie and the rest of the ladies.

Fortunately the matter was treated as a joke, and we all laughed; but it was a dangerous experiment, and I felt very uneasy for a moment as to the result. I subsequently referred to the matter to Carrie, but she said: 'Oh, he's not much more than a boy.' I said that he had a very large moustache for a boy. Carrie replied: 'I didn't say he was not a nice boy.'

December 26. I did not sleep very well last night; I never do in a strange bed. I feel a little indigestion, which one must expect at this time of the year. Carrie and I returned to Town in the evening. Lupin came in late. He said he enjoyed his Christmas, and added: 'I feel as fit as a Lowther Arcade fiddle, and only require a little more "oof" to feel as fit as a £500 Stradivarius.' I have long since given up trying to understand Lupin's slang, or asking him to explain it.

A Christmas Day
Swim in the
Serpentine

For 250 years Londoners have been heading for the Serpentine in Hyde Park in order to cool off during hot city summers. However, a group of intrepid swimmers don't limit themselves to the summer months only, but brave hoar frost and shrieking winter winds to take a daily dip throughout the

Christmas 1938 Peter Pan Cup 100 yds race at the Serpentine

year. Even when the lake is frozen over it doesn't prevent members of the club from effecting entry. Bearing a pickaxe in hand they will hack through the ice in order to splash about in water of sub-zero temperatures.

These resolute masochists are members of the Serpentine Swimming Club which was established in 1864 and is the oldest surviving swimming club in Britain. They are perhaps best known for their daring Christmas morning swim, an annual event which grabbed the public's attention in the twenties when James Barrie, whose Peter Pan is commemorated by a bronze statue in nearby Kensington Gardens, joined the club and established the Peter Pan Cup which was to be given to the winner of the Christmas Day one hundred yards handicapped race.

from

The Accounts of the Inner Temple, London, 1562

At the Inns of Court during the sixteenth and seventeenth centuries Christmas revelling of a costly and elaborate

kind was at the centre of social activities, although the extent to which an Inn was prepared to go naturally varied from year to year. Sometimes an outbreak of plague dispersed the officers and students, or sometimes the number remaining in residence during the vacation made it difficult to mount an elaborate spectacle despite rules and heavy fines designed to discourage absenteeism. 1562, however, seems to have been a year for 'grand' celebration.

Christmas Eve

At the first course the minstrels must sound their instruments and go before, and the Steward and Marshall are next to follow together, and after them the Gentleman Server, and then cometh the meat. Those three officers are to make altogether three solemn curtsies at three several times between the screen and the upper table, beginning with the first at the end of the Benchers' table, the second at the midst, and the third at the other end; and then standing by, the server performeth his office.

When the first table is set and served, the Steward's table is next to be served; after him, the Masters' table of the Revels; then that of the Master of the Game; the high Constable-Marshall; then the Lieutenant of the Tower; then the Utter Barristers' table; and lastly the Clerks' table. All which time the musicians must stand right above the hearth side, with the noise of their music, their faces direct towards the highest table, and that done, to return into the Buttery with their music sounding.

At the second course every table is to be served as at the first course in every respect; which performed, the servitors and musicians are to resort to the place assigned for them to dine at, which is the valets' or yeomans' table beneath the screen. Dinner ended, the musicians prepare to sing a song at the

Boar's Head – A Cavalier Christmas

highest table, which ceremony accomplished, then the officers are to address themselves, everyone in his office, to avoid [*clear*] the tables in fair and decent manner, they beginning at the Clerks' table, thence proceed to the next, and thence to all the others till the highest table be solemnly avoided.

Then after a little repose, the persons at the highest table arise, and prepare to revels, in which time the Butlers and other servitors with them are to dine in the Library.

At both the doors in the Hall [*i.e. the doors in the screen*] are porters to view the comers in and out at meal times. To each of them is allowed a cast of bread and a candle nightly after supper.

At night before supper, are revels and dancing, and so also after supper during the twelve days of Christmas. The ancientest Master of the Revels is after dinner and supper to sing a carol or song, and command other gentlemen then there present to sing with him and the Company, and so it is very decently performed.

· *A London Christmas* ·

Christmas Day

Service in the Church ended, the gentlemen presently repair
into the Hall to breakfast, with brawn, mustard and malmsy.

At dinner the Butler appointed for grand Christmas is to see
the tables covered and furnished . . . At the first course is
served in a fair and large boar's head, upon a silver platter,
with minstralsy. Two gentlemen in gowns are to attend at
supper, and to bear two fair torches of wax next before the
musicians and trumpeters, and stand above the fire with the
music, till the first course be served in through the Hall.
Which performed, they with the music are to return into the
Buttery. The like course is to be observed in all things during
the time of Christmas. The like at supper.

At service time this evening the two youngest butlers are to
bear two torches in the Genealogia. A repast at dinner is 12d
which strangers of worth are admitted to take in the Hall, and
such are to be placed at the discretion of the Marshall.

St Stephen's Day [Boxing Day]

The Butler appointed for Christmas is to see the tables
covered . . . Young gentlemen of the House are to attend and
serve till the latter dinner, and then dine themselves.

This day, the Server, Carver and Cup-bearer are to serve as
afore. After the first course served in, the Constable-Marshall
cometh into the Hall, arranged with a fair, rich, complete
harness, white and bright and gilt, with a nest of feathers of all
colours upon his crest or helm, and a gilt pole-axe in his hand;
to whom is associate the Lieutenant of the Tower, armed with
a fair white armour, a nest of feathers in his helm, and a like
pole-axe in his hand; and with them sixteen trumpeters, four
drums and fifes going in rank before them. And with them
attend four men in white harness from the middle upwards,
and halberds in their hands, bearing on their shoulders the

Tower; which persons with the drums, trumpets and music, go three times about the fire. Then the Constable-Marshall, after two or three curtseys made, kneeleth down before the Lord Chancellor; behind him the Lieutenant; and they kneeling, the Constable-Marshall pronounceth an oration of a quarter of an hour's length, thereby declaring the purpose of his coming; and that his purpose is to be admitted into his Lordship's service.

The Lord Chancellor saith that he will take further advice therein.

Then the Constable-Marshall standing up, in submissive manner delivereth his naked sword to the Steward, who giveth it to the Lord Chancellor. And thereupon the Lord Chancellor willeth the Marshall to place the Constable-Marshall in his seat; and so he doth, with the Lieutenant also in his seat or place. During this ceremony the Tower is placed beneath the fire.

Then cometh in the Master of the Game apparelled in green velvet, and the Ranger of the Forest also, in a green suit of satin, bearing in his hand a green bow and divers arrows, with either of them a hunting horn about their necks. Blowing together three blasts of venery, they pace round about the fire three times. Then the Master of the Game makes three curtseys, as aforesaid, and kneeleth down before the Lord Chancellor, declaring the cause of his coming, and desireth to be admitted into his service, etc. All this time the Ranger of the Forest standeth directly behind him. Then the Master of the Game standeth up.

This ceremony also performed, a Huntsman cometh into the Hall with a fox and a purse-net; with a cat, both bound at the end of a staff; and with them nine or ten couple of hounds, with the blowing of hunting horns. And the fox and the cat are by the hounds set upon and killed beneath the fire. This sport finished, the Marshall placeth them in their several appointed places.

Then proceedeth the second course, which done and served out, the Common Sergeant delivereth a plausible speech to the Lord Chancellor and his company at the highest table, how necessary a thing it is to have officers at this present, the Constable-Marshall and the Master of the Game, for the better honour and reputation of the Commonwealth, and wisheth them to be received etc.

Then the King's Serjeant at law declareth and inferreth the necessity; which heard, the Lord Chancellor desireth respite of further advice. Then the ancientest of the Masters of the Revels singeth a song, with the assistance of others there present.

At supper the Hall is to be served in all solemnity, as upon Christmas Day both the first and second course to the highest table. Supper ended, the Constable-Marshall presenteth himself with drums before him, mounted upon a scaffold borne by four men and goeth three times round about the hearth, crying out aloud, *A Lord! A Lord!* etc. Then he descendeth and goeth to dance etc., and after he calleth his court, everyone by name, one by one in this manner.

Sir Francis Flatterer of Fowleshurst, in the County of Buckingham.

Sir Randle Rackabite of Rascal Hall, in the County of Rakehell.

Sir Morgan Mumchance of Muck Monkery, in the County of Mad Popery.

Sir Bartholomew Baldbreech of Buttocksbury, in the County of Breakneck.

This done, the Lord of Misrule addresseth himself to the banquet, which ended with some minstrelsy, mirth and dancing, every man departeth to rest.

Christmas Day in the Workhouse

GEORGE R. SIMS

George R. Sims lived in London all his life. Like so many writers of his day he started out as a journalist, although his father tried to prevent his scribbling by placing him in his office and instructing him in the mysteries of commerce. He spent a great deal of his spare time roaming around the city in order to collect material for a series of special articles he wrote for the Daily News *called 'Horrible London'.*

He was also a dramatist and poet and Christmas Day in the Workhouse, *published in 1877, is a classic example of Victorian popular art. The sentimental tone of his poem parodies the extreme austerity of Christmas Day celebrations in the workhouse. Whereas the Dickensian spirit had been one of general good will, in the latter part of the nineteenth century Christmas charities took the opportunity to preach moral reform. The respectable poor were considered deserving while those who gave way to drinking or disorderly behaviour were not.*

It is Christmas Day in the Workhouse,
And the cold bare walls are bright
With garlands of green and holly,
And the place is a pleasant sight:

· *A London Christmas* ·

For with clean-washed hands and faces,
In a long and hungry line
The paupers sit at the tables
For this is the hour they dine.

And the guardians and their ladies
Although the wind is east,
Have come in their furs and wrappers,
To watch their charges feast;
To smile and be condescending,
Put pudding on pauper plates,
To be hosts at the workhouse banquet
They've paid for — with the rates.

Oh, the paupers are meek and lowly
With their 'Thank'ee kindly, mum's'
So long as they fill their stomachs,
What matter it whence it comes?
But one of the old men mutters,
And pushes his plate aside:
'Great God!' he cries, 'but it chokes me!
For this is the day *she* died.'

The guardians gazed in horror,
The master's face went white;
'Did a pauper refuse the pudding?'
'Could their ears believe aright?'
Then the ladies clutched their husbands,
Thinking the man would die,
Struck by a bolt, or something,
By the outraged One on high.

But the pauper sat for a moment,
Then rose 'mid a silence grim,

The Poor at Christmas, 1850s

For the others had ceased to chatter
And trembled in every limb.
He looked at the guardians' ladies,
Then, eyeing their lords, he said,
'I eat not the food of villains
Whose hands are foul and red:

'Whose victims cry for vengeance
From their dank, unhallowed graves.'
'He's drunk!' said the workhouse master,
'Or else he's mad and raves.'
'Not drunk or mad,' cried the pauper,
'But only a hunted beast,
Who, torn by the hounds and mangled,
Declines the vulture's feast.

71

· *A London Christmas* ·

'I care not a curse for the guardians,
And I won't be dragged away.
Just let me have the fit out,
It's only Christmas Day
That the black past comes to goad me,
And prey on my burning brain;
I'll tell you the rest in a whisper, –
I swear I won't shout again.

'Keep your hands off me, curse you!
Hear me right out to the end.
You come here to see how paupers
The season of Christmas spend.
You come here to watch us feeding,
As they watch the captured beast.
Hear why a penniless pauper
Spits on your paltry feast.

'Do you think I will take your bounty,
And let you smile and think
You're doing a noble action
With the parish's meat and drink?
Where is my wife, you traitors –
The poor old wife you slew?
Yes, by the God above us,
My Nance was killed by you!

'Last winter my wife lay dying,
Starved in a filthy den;
I had never been to the parish –
I came to the parish then.
I swallowed my pride in coming,
For, ere the ruin came,

Street Urchin at Christmas by Augustus E. Mulready

I held up my head as a trader.
And I bore a spotless name.

'I came to the parish, craving
Bread for a starving wife,
Bread for the woman who'd loved me
Through fifty years of life;
And what do you think they told me,
Mocking my awful grief?
That "the House" was open to us,
But they wouldn't give "out relief".

73

· *A London Christmas* ·

Children's Christmas Party

'I slunk to the filthy alley –
'Twas a cold, raw Christmas eve –
And the baker's shops were open,
Tempting a man to thieve;
But I clenched my fists together,
Holding my head awry,
So I came to her empty-handed
And mournfully told her why.

'Then I told her "the House" was open;
She had heard of the ways of *that*,
For her bloodless cheeks went crimson,
And up in her rags she sat,
Crying, "Bide the Christmas here, John,
We've never had one apart;

74

I think I can bear the hunger, –
The other would break my heart."

'All through that eve I watched her,
Holding her hand in mine,
Praying the Lord, and weeping,
Till my lips were salt as brine.
I asked her once if she hungered,
And as she answered "No,"
The moon shone in at the window
Set in a wreath of snow.

'Then the room was bathed in glory,
And I saw in my darling's eyes
The far-away look of wonder
That comes when the spirit flies;
And her lips were parched and parted,
And her reason came and went,
For she raved of our home in Devon,
Where our happiest years were spent.

'And the accents long forgotten,
Came back to the tongue once more,
For she talked like the country lassie
I woo'd by the Devon shore.
Then she rose to her feet and trembled,
And fell on the rags and moaned,
And, "Give me a crust – I'm famished –
For the love of God!" she groaned.

'I rushed from the room like a madman,
And flew to the workhouse gate,
Crying, "Food for a dying woman!"
And the answer came, "Too late."

75

· *A London Christmas* ·

They drove me away with curses;
Then I fought with a dog in the street,
And tore from the mongrel's clutches
A crust he was trying to eat.

'Back through the filthy by-lanes!
Back, through the trampled slush!
Up to the crazy garret,
Wrapped in an awful hush.
My heart sank down at the threshold,
And I paused with a sudden thrill,
For there in the silv'ry moonlight
My Nance lay, cold and still.

'Up to the blackened ceiling
The sunken eyes were cast –
I knew on those lips all bloodless
My name had been the last;
She'd called for her absent husband –
O God! had I but known! –
Had called in vain, and in anguish
Had died in that den – alone.

'Yes, there in a land of plenty,
Lay a loving woman dead,
Cruelly starved and murdered
For a loaf of the parish bread.
At yonder gate, last Christmas,
I craved for a human life.
You, who would feast us paupers,
What of my murdered wife!

'There, get ye gone to your dinners;
Don't mind me in the least;

Think of the happy paupers
Eating your Christmas feast;
And when you recount their blessings
In your smug parochial way,
Say what you did for *me*, too,
Only last Christmas Day.'

Sir Roger de Coverley on Christmas

JOSEPH ADDISON

The gentlest and most humane satire of the early eighteenth century is to be found in Joseph Addison's work for the Spectator *which was intended to 'bring philosophy out of the closets'. Among the many imaginary characters who voiced their opinions on these pages was Sir Roger de Coverley, on the one hand a simple country gentleman come to town, and on the other a feudal character confronted with modern ways. His views on the subject of Christmas were given to readers on 8 January 1712.*

· A London Christmas ·

I was no sooner come into Gray's Inn walks, but I heard my friend upon the terrace hemming twice or thrice to himself with great vigour, for he loves to clear his pipes in good air (to make use of his own phrase), and is not a little pleased with anyone who takes notice of the strength which he still exerts in morning hems. I was touched with a secret joy at the sight of the good old man, who before he saw me was engaged in conversation with a beggar man that had asked an alms of him. I could hear my friend chide him for not finding out some work; but at the same time saw him put his hand into his pocket and give him sixpence.

Our salutations were very hearty on both sides, consisting of many kinds of shakes of the hand, and several affectionate looks which we cast upon one another. He afterwards fell into an account of the diversions which had passed in his house during the holidays; for Sir Roger, after the laudable custom of his ancestors, always keeps open house at Christmas. I learned from him, that he had killed eight fat hogs for this season; that he had dealt about his chines very liberally amongst his neighbours; and that in particular he had sent a string of hog's-puddings with a pack of cards to every poor family in the parish. 'I have often thought', says Sir Roger, 'it happens very well that Christmas should fall out in the middle of winter. It is the most dead and uncomfortable time of the year, when the poor people would suffer very much from their poverty and cold, if they had not good cheer, warm fires, and Christmas gambols to support them. I love to rejoice their poor hearts at this season, and to see the whole village merry in my great hall. I allow a double quantity of malt to my small beer, and set it a-running for twelve days to every one that calls for it. I have always a piece of cold beef and a mince-pie upon the table, and am wonderfully pleased to see my tenants pass away a whole evening in playing their innocent tricks, and smutting one another. Our friend Will Wimble is as merry as any of

them, and shows a thousand roguish tricks upon these occasions.'

I was very much delighted with the reflection of my old friend, which carried so much goodness in it.

from

As I Please

GEORGE ORWELL

This article was published on 20 December 1946 in the Socialist weekly Tribune *of which Orwell at the time was literary editor. With the 'As I Please' series his journalism became more personal, covering an immense variety of subjects. In this particular piece he justifies general debauchery at Christmas, and admonishes vegetarians and teetotallers for their moralistic attitude, while at the same time recognizing that in war-torn Europe thousands were having to do without.*

An advertisement in my Sunday paper sets forth in the form of a picture the four things that are needed for a successful Christmas. At the top of the picture is a roast turkey; below that, a Christmas pudding; below that, a dish of mince pies; and below that, a tin of —'s Liver Salt.

· A London Christmas ·

It is a simple recipe for happiness. First the meal, then the antidote, then another meal. The ancient Romans were the great masters of this technique. However, having just looked up the word *vomitorium* in the Latin dictionary, I find that after all it does *not* mean a place where you went to be sick after dinner. So perhaps this was not a normal feature of every Roman home, as is commonly believed.

Implied in the above-mentioned advertisement is the notion that a good meal means a meal at which you overeat yourself. In principle I agree. I only add in passing that when we gorge ourselves this Christmas, if we do get the chance to gorge ourselves, it is worth giving a thought to the thousand million human beings, or thereabouts, who will be doing no such thing. For in the long run our Christmas dinners would be safer if we could make sure that everyone else had a Christmas dinner as well. But I will come back to that presently.

The only reasonable motive for not overeating at Christmas would be that somebody else needs the food more than you do. A deliberately austere Christmas would be an absurdity. The whole point of Christmas is that it is a debauch — as it was probably long before the birth of Christ was arbitrarily fixed at that date. Children know this very well. From their point of view Christmas is not a day of temperate enjoyment, but of fierce pleasures which they are quite willing to pay for with a certain amount of pain. The awakening at about 4 a.m. to inspect your stockings; the quarrels over toys all through the morning, and the exciting whiffs of mincemeat and sage-and-onions escaping from the kitchen door; the battle with enormous platefuls of turkey, and the pulling of the wishbone; the darkening of the windows and the entry of the flaming plum pudding; the hurry to make sure that everyone has a piece on his plate while the brandy is still alight; the momentary panic when it is rumoured that Baby has swallowed the threepenny bit; the stupor all through the

Harrod's Meathall, Christmas 1929

afternoon; the Christmas cake with almond icing an inch thick; the peevishness next morning and the castor oil on December 27th – it is an up-and-down business, by no means all pleasant, but well worth while for the sake of its more dramatic moments.

Teetotallers and vegetarians are always scandalized by this attitude. As they see it, the only rational objective is to avoid pain and to stay alive as long as possible. If you refrain from drinking alcohol, or eating meat, or whatever it is, you may expect to live an extra five years, while if you overeat or overdrink you will pay for it in acute physical pain on the following day. Surely it follows that all excesses, even a one-a-year outbreak such as Christmas, should be avoided as a matter of course?

Actually it doesn't follow at all. One may decide, with full knowledge of what one is doing, that an occasional good time is worth the damage it inflicts on one's liver. For health is not the only thing that matters: friendship, hospitality, and the heightened spirits and change of outlook that one gets by eating and drinking in good company are also valuable. I doubt whether, on balance, even outright drunkenness does harm, provided it is infrequent — twice a year, say. The whole experience, including the repentance afterwards, makes a sort of break in one's mental routine, comparable to a week-end in a foreign country, which is probably beneficial.

In all ages men have realized this. There is a wide consensus of opinion, stretching back to the days before the alphabet, that whereas habitual soaking is bad, conviviality is good, even if one does sometimes feel sorry for it next morning. How enormous is the literature of eating and drinking, especially drinking, and how little that is worth while has been said on the other side! Offhand I can't remember a single poem in praise of water, i.e. water regarded as a drink. It is hard to imagine what one could say about it. It quenches thirst: that is the end of the story. As for poems in praise of wine, on the other hand even the surviving ones would fill a shelf of books. The poets started turning them out on the very day when the fermentation of the grape was first discovered. Whisky, brandy and other distilled liquors have been less eloquently praised, partly because they came later in time. But beer has had quite a good press, starting well back in the Middle Ages, long before anyone had learned to put hops in it. Curiously enough, I can't remember a poem in praise of stout, not even draught stout, which is better than the bottled variety, in my opinion. There is an extremely disgusting description in *Ulysses* of the stout-vats in Dublin. But there is a sort of back-handed tribute to stout in the fact that this description, though widely known, has not done much towards putting the Irish off their favourite drink.

· A London Christmas ·

The literature of eating is also large, though mostly in prose. But in all the writers who have enjoyed describing food, from Rabelais to Dickens and from Petronius to Mrs Beeton, I cannot remember a single passage which puts dietetic considerations first. Always food is felt to be an end in itself. No one has written memorable prose about vitamins, or the dangers of excess of proteins, or the importance of masticating everything thirty-two times. All in all, there seems to be a heavy weight of testimony on the side of overeating and overdrinking, provided always that they take place on recognized occasions and not too frequently.

But ought we to overeat and overdrink this Christmas? We ought not to, nor will most of us get the opportunity. I am writing in praise of Christmas, but in praise of Christmas 1947, or perhaps 1948. The world as a whole is not exactly in a condition for festivities this year. Between the Rhine and the Pacific there cannot be very many people who are in need of —'s Liver Salt. In India there are, and always have been, about 10 million people who only get one square meal a day. In China, conditions are no doubt much the same. In Germany, Austria, Greece and elsewhere, scores of millions of people are existing on a diet which keeps breath in the body but leaves no strength for work. All over the war-wrecked areas from Brussels to Stalingrad, other uncounted millions are living in the cellars of bombed houses, in hide-outs in the forests, or in squalid huts behind barbed wire. It is not so pleasant to read almost simultaneously that a large proportion of our Christmas turkeys will come from Hungary, and that the Hungarian writers and journalists – presumably not the worst-paid section of the community – are in such desperate straits that they would be glad to receive presents of saccharine and cast-off clothing from English sympathizers. In such circumstances we could hardly have a 'proper' Christmas, even if the materials for it existed.

But we will have one sooner or later, in 1947, or 1948, or maybe even in 1949. And when we do, may there be no gloomy voices of vegetarians or teetotallers to lecture us about the things that we are doing to the linings of our stomachs. One celebrates a feast for its own sake, and not for any supposed benefit to the lining of one's stomach. Meanwhile Christmas is here, or nearly. Santa Claus is rounding up his reindeer, the postman staggers from door to door beneath his bulging sack of Christmas cards, the black markets are humming, and Britain has imported over 7,000 crates of mistletoe from France. So I wish everyone an old-fashioned Christmas in 1947, and meanwhile, half a turkey, three tangerines, and a bottle of whisky at not more than double the legal price.

London Fare

By the end of the eighteenth century the additional food which people demanded at Christmas was an important source of trade, and the season, according to the *London Magazine* was 'held sacred by good eating and drinking'. With about three hundred thousand inhabitants, London got its supplies from the surrounding countryside for the traditional Christmas dinner of turkey, plum-porridge and mince pies – though the popularity of the mine pie seemed temporarily marred in 1736 when the *London Magazine* declared that, 'the excellent and most noble Christmas pie, usually prepared with the art of meer Force and Female Philosophy was giving way to the ragous and kickshaws of a fanatical kingdom – or rather French pastries'.

Mrs Glasse's popular cookery book was used by many Londoners in the mid-eighteenth century:

Mrs Glasse's Plum-Porridge Recipe

Take a leg and shin of beef, put them into eight gallons of water, and boil them till they are very tender, and when the broth is strong strain it out; wipe the pot and put in the broth again; then slice six penny-loaves thin, cut off the top and bottom, put some of the liquor to it, cover it up and let it stand a quarter of an hour, boil it and strain it, and then put it into your pot, let it boil a quarter of an hour, then put in five pounds of currants, clean washed and picked; let them boil a little, and put in five pounds of raisons of the sun stoned, and two pounds of prunes, and let them boil till they swell, then put in three quarters of an ounce of mace, half an ounce of cloves, two nutmegs, all of them beat fine, and mix it with a little liquor cold, and put them in a very little while, and take off the pot, then put in three pounds of sugar, a little salt, a quart of sack, a quart of claret, and the juice of two or three lemons. You may thicken with sago instead of bread (if you please); pour them into earthen pan, and keep them for use.

During this period good cooking was considered an art. Chefs were in demand and learning the basic skills was a matter taken seriously by both men and women, as the following advertisement shows:

E. Kidder's Receipts of Pastry and Cookery
for the use of his scholars
who teaches at his school in

· *A London Christmas* ·

Queen Street near St Thomas Apostles
On Mondays, Tuesdays and Wednesdays
In the afternoon
Also
On Thursdays, Fridays and Saturdays
In the afternoon
at his School next to
Furnivals Inn Holburn.
Ladies may be taught at
their own houses.

E. Kidder's Famous Recipe for Plum Cake

Take 6 pnd of currants, 5 pnd of flower, an ounce of cloves and mace, a little cinnamon, ½ an ounce of netmegs, ½ a pnd of pounded and blanch'd almonds, ½ a pnd of sugar, 3 quartrs of a pnd of slic'd citron, lemon and orange peel, ½ a pint of sack, a little honey water and a quart of ale; a quart of cream, 2 pnd and ½ of butter melted and pour'd into the middle thereof; then strain strew a little flower thereon and let it lye to rise, then work it well together, than lay it before the fire to rise; work it up till it is very smooth, then put it in an hoop with a paper flower'd at the bottom.

In the fifteenth and sixteenth centuries the flourishing City Livery Companies celebrated Christmas to the full, as this recipe for a Christmas Pie shows, found in the records of the Salters' Company and dating from the reign of Richard II:

Take pheasant, hare and chicken or capon, of each one; with two partridges, two pigeons and two coneys; and smite them in pieces and pick clean away therefrom all the bones that you may; and therewith do them into a crust of good paste, made craftily in the likeness of a bird's body with the

livers and hearts, two kidneys of sheep, and forcemeat and
eggs made into balls. Cast thereto powder of pepper, salt,
spice, vinegar and mushrooms pickled, and then take the
bones and let them seethe in a pot to make a good broth
there for, and do it into the crust of paste, and close it up
fast, and bake it well and so serve it forth; with the head of
one of the birds stuck at the one end of the crust, and a great
tail at the other, and divers of his long feathers set in
cunningly all about him.

from

The Unclassed

GEORGE GISSING

*Like so many of his Northern contemporaries George
Gissing moved to London from his home town of Wakefield
in 1877 to try his hand at earning a living as a writer.
His struggle to be recognized and to earn the bare
minimum living wage is reflected in the gloomy pessimism
of his polemical working-class novels. The two types of
Christmas described here in his second novel,* The
Unclassed, *are characteristically gloomy. In one household an uncle chooses the solemn occasion to elicit a promise
from his nephew concerning the future care of his daughter,*

· A London Christmas ·

*and in the other an aunt explains to her young niece why
merry-making at Christmas is a sin.*

Sarah took Harriet to bed early. Julian had got hold of his
Plutarch again, and read snatches of it aloud every now and
then. His uncle paid no heed, was sunk in dull reverie. When
they had sat thus for more than an hour, Mr Smales began to
exhibit a wish to talk.

'Put the book away, and draw up to the fire, my boy,' he
said, with as near an approach to heartiness as he was capable
of. 'It's Christmas time, and Christmas only comes once a
year.'

He rubbed his palms together, then began to twist the
corners of his handkerchief.

'Well, Julian,' he went on, leaning feebly forward to the
fire, 'a year more school, I suppose, and then – business;
what?'

'Yes, uncle.'

The boy spoke cheerfully, but yet not in the same natural
way as before.

'I wish I could afford to make you something better, my lad;
you ought to be something better by rights. And I don't well
know what you'll find to do in this little shop. The business
might be better; yes, might be better. You won't have much
practice in dispensing, I'm afraid, unless things improve. It is
mostly hair-oil, – and the patent medicines. It's a poor
look-out for you, Julian.'

There was a silence.

'Harriet isn't quite well yet, is she?' Smales went on, half to
himself.

'No, she looked poorly tonight.'

'Julian,' began the other, but paused, rubbing his hands
more nervously than ever.

'Yes, uncle?'

Penny Postage Jubilee Print

'I wonder what 'ud become of her if I – if I died now? You're growing up, and you're a clever lad; you'll soon be able to shift for yourself. And I shall have nothing to leave either her or you, Julian – nothing, – nothing! She'll have to get her living somehow. I must think of some easy business for her, I must. She might be a teacher, but her head isn't strong enough, I fear. Julian —'

'Yes, uncle?'

'You – you are old enough to understand things, my boy,' went on his uncle, with quavering voice. 'Suppose, after I'm dead and gone, Harriet should want help. She won't make many friends, I fear, and she'll have bad health. Suppose she was in want of any kind, – you'd stand by her, Julian, wouldn't you? You'd be a friend to her, – always?'

'Indeed I would, uncle!' exclaimed the boy stoutly.

'You promise me that, Julian, this Christmas night? – you promise it?'

'Yes, I promise, uncle. You've always been kind and good to me, and see if I'm not the same to Harriet.'

His voice trembled with generous emotion.

'No, I shan't see it, my boy,' said Smales, shaking his head drearily; 'but the promise will be a comfort to me at the end, a comfort to me. You're a good lad, Julian!'

Silence came upon them again.

*　　*　　*

In the same district, in one of a row of semi-detached houses standing in gardens, lived Ida's little friend, Maud Enderby, with her aunt, Miss Bygrave, a lady of forty-two or forty-three. The rooms were small and dark; the furniture sparse, old-fashioned, and much worn; there were no ornaments in any of the rooms, with the exception of a few pictures representing the saddest incidents in the life of Christ. On entering the front door you were oppressed by the chill, damp atmosphere, and by a certain unnatural stillness. The stairs were not carpeted, but stained a dark colour; a footfall upon them, however light, echoed strangely as if from empty chambers above. There was no sign of lack of repair; perfect order and cleanliness wherever the eye penetrated; yet the general effect was an unspeakable desolation.

Maud Enderby, on reaching home after her meeting with Ida, entered the front parlour, and sat down in silence near the window, where faint daylight yet glimmered. The room was without fire. Over the mantelpiece hung an engraving of the Crucifixion; on the opposite wall were the Agony in the Garden, and an Entombment; all after old masters. The centre table, a few chairs, and a small sideboard were the sole articles of furniture. The table was spread with a white cloth; upon it were a loaf of bread, a pitcher containing milk, two plates, and two glasses.

Maud sat in the cold room for a quarter of an hour; it became quite dark. Then was heard a soft footstep descending the stairs; the door opened, and a lady came in, bearing a lighted lamp, which she stood upon the table. She was tall, very slender, and with a face which a painter might have used to personify the spiritual life. Its outlines were of severe perfection; its expression a confirmed grief, subdued by, and made subordinate to, the consciousness of an inward strength which could convert suffering into triumph. Her garment was black, of the simplest possible design. In looking at Maud, as the child rose from the chair, it was scarcely affection that her eyes expressed, rather a grave compassion. Maud took a seat at the table without speaking; her aunt sat down over against her. In perfect silence they partook of the milk and the bread. Miss Bygrave then cleared the table with her own hands, and took the things out of the room. Maud still kept her place. The child's manner was not at all constrained; she was evidently behaving in her wonted way. Her eyes wandered about the room with rather a dreamy gaze, and, as often as they fell upon her aunt's face, became very serious, though in no degree expressive of fear or even awe.

Miss Bygrave returned, and seated herself near the little girl; then remained thoughtful for some minutes. The breath from their lips was plainly visible on the air. Maud almost shivered now and then, but forced herself to suppress the impulse. Her aunt presently broke the silence, speaking in a low voice, which had nothing of tenderness, but was most impressive in its earnest calm.

'I wish to speak to you before you go upstairs, Maud; to speak of things which you cannot understand fully as yet, but which you are old enough to begin to think about.'

Maud was surprised. It was the first time that her aunt had ever addressed her in this serious way. She was used to being all but ignored, though never in a manner which made her feel that she was treated unkindly. There was nothing like confidence between them; only in care for her bodily wants did Miss Bygrave fill the place of the mother whose affection the child had never known. Maud crossed her hands on her lap, and looked up with respectful attention upon her pale sweet little face.

'Do you wonder at all,' Miss Bygrave went on, 'why we never spend Christmas like your friends do in their homes, with eating and drinking and all sorts of merriment?'

'Yes, aunt, I do.'

It was evidently the truth, and given with the simple directness which characterised the child.

'You know what Christmas Day means, Maud?'

'It is the day on which Christ was born.'

'And for what purpose did Christ come as a child on earth?'

Maud thought for a moment. She had never had any direct religious teaching; all she knew of these matters was gathered from her regular attendance at church. She replied in a phrase

which had rested in her mind, though probably conveying little if any meaning to her.

'He came to make us free from sin.'

'And so we should rejoice at His coming. But would it please Him, do you think, to see us showing our joy by indulging in those very sins from which He came to free us?'

Maud looked with puzzled countenance.

'Is it a sin to like cake and sweet things, aunt?'

The gravity of the question brought a smile to Miss Bygrave's close, strong lips.

'Listen, Maud,' she said, 'and I will tell you what I mean. For you to like such things is no sin, as long as you are still too young to have it explained to you why you should overcome that liking. As I said, you are now old enough to begin to think of more than a child's foolishness, to ask yourself what is the meaning of the life which has been given you, what duties you must set before yourself as you grow up to be a woman. When once these duties have become clear to you, when you understand what the end of life is, and how you should seek to gain it, then many things become sinful which were not so before, and many duties must be performed which previously you were not ready for.'

Miss Bygrave spoke with effort, as if she found it difficult to express herself in sufficiently simple phraseology. Speaking, she did not look at the child; and, when the pause came, her eyes were still fixed absently on the picture above the mantelpiece.

'Keep in mind what I shall tell you,' she proceeded with growing solemnity, 'and some day you will better understand its meaning than you can now. The sin which Christ came to free us from was – fondness for the world, enjoyment of what we call pleasure, desire for happiness on earth. He Himself came to set us the example of one to whom the world was nothing, who could put aside every joy, and make His life a life of sorrows. Even that was not enough. When the time had

93

come, and He had finished His teaching of the disciples whom He chose, He willingly underwent the most cruel of all deaths, to prove that His teaching had been the truth, and to show us that we must face any most dreadful suffering rather than desert what we believe to be right.'

She pointed to the crucified figure, and Maud followed the direction of her hand with awed gaze.

'And this,' said Miss Bygrave, 'is why I think it wrong to make Christmas a time of merriment. In the true Christian, every enjoyment which comes from the body is a sin. If you feel you *like* this or that, it is a sign that you must renounce it, give it up. If you feel fond of life, you must force yourself to hate it; for life is sin. Life is given to us that we may conquer ourselves. We are placed in the midst of sin that we may struggle against its temptations. There is temptation in the very breath you draw, since you feel a dread if it is checked. You must live so as to be ready at any moment to give up your life with gladness, as a burden which it has been appointed you to bear for a time. There is temptation in the love you feel for those around you; it makes you cling to life; you are tempted to grieve if you lose them, whereas death is the greatest blessing in the gift of God. And just because it is so, we must not snatch at it before our time; it would be a sin to kill ourselves, since that would be to escape from the tasks set us. Many pleasures would seem to be innocent, but even these it is better to renounce, since for that purpose does every pleasure exist. I speak of the pleasures of the world. One joy there is which we may and must pursue, the joy of sacrifice. The more the body suffers, the greater should be the delight of the soul; and the only moment of perfect happiness should be that when the world grows dark around us, and we feel the hand of death upon our hearts.'

She was silent, and both sat in the cold room without word or motion.

Norway's Gift to Trafalgar Square

One sight that has become familiar to all Londoners at Christmas is the Norwegian Christmas tree given annually to the people of Westminster as a token of their courage during the Blitz. It is placed among the fountains of Trafalgar Square and has become one of the most attractive sights of London in December.

It was first sent in 1947 from the City of Oslo as a mark of appreciation for British friendship given to King Haakon VII who escaped here when Norway was invaded in 1940, and as a gesture of thanks for the hospitality given to the Norwegian Government which set up in exile in London. The tree was also intended to be a symbol of peace and reconciliation with hundreds of white lights illuminating the dark December evenings.

The tradition originated during the war, when every year Norwegian commandos would bring back from Norway a tree as a gift for their king in exile, and it is a custom that has endured until today. Whereas the Christmas tree that Prince Albert introduced to this country was a domestic one to be set up by the fire place or in the front window of a family home, the Norwegian tree was specifically given for the benefit of the entire British people and therefore established a new tradition of setting up civic and communal trees in squares and outside public buildings as public recognition of the season.

Measuring up to thirty-six feet high and being perhaps sixty

Norwegian Christmas Tree, Trafalgar Square

or seventy years in age, the tree is supposed to be the tallest spruce found in Norway each year. After being felled the tree is then transported across the North Sea to Felixstowe where it continues its journey by road to Trafalgar Square.

Of course over the years there are bound to have been a few accidents. For instance, on one occasion the tree snapped in half when it was being off-loaded, prompting the people of Norway to send an immediate substitute. And on another occasion winds broke ten feet off the tip of the tree once it had been put in place. Not even the 1973 power workers' strike prevented the illumination of the tree, although admittedly it was lit up for only a few hours before being plunged into darkness by the cuts.

from

London Labour and London Poor

HENRY MAYHEW

Mayhew was the joint editor of the humorous weekly
Punch, *but his real fame comes from a work of
astonishing detail and research based on interviews with
working-class people, issued in twopenny numbers between
1851 and 1862. The aim of the work, said Mayhew,
was to form 'a cyclopaedia of the industry, the want, and
the vice of the great Metropolis', which he hoped would,
'give the rich a more intimate knowledge of the sufferings,
and frequent heroism under those sufferings, of the poor.'
This extract deals with the commercial side of Christmas
in terms of produce, cost and labour.*

Of Christmasing – Laurel, Ivy, Holly, and Mistletoe

In London a large trade is carried on in 'Christmasing,' or in
the sale of holly and mistletoe, for Christmas sports and
decorations. I have appended a table of the quantity of these
'branches' sold, nearly 250,000, and of the money expended
upon them in the streets. It must be borne in mind, to account
for this expenditure for a brief season, that almost every

housekeeper will expend something in 'Christmasing;' from 2*d.* to 1*s.* 6*d.*, and the poor buy a pennyworth, or a halfpennyworth each, and they are the coster's customers. In some houses, which are let off in rooms, floors, or suites of apartments, and not to the poorest class, every room will have the cheery decoration of holly, its bright, and as if *glazed* leaves and red berries, reflecting the light from fire or candle. 'Then, look,' said a gardener to me, 'what's spent on a-Christmasing the churches! Why, now, properly to Christmas St Paul's, I say *properly*, mind, would take 50*l.* worth at least; aye, more, when I think of it, nearer 100*l.* I hope there'll be no "No Popery" nonsense against Christmasing this year. I'm always sorry when anything of that kind's afloat, because it's frequently a hindrance to business.' This was said three weeks before Christmas. In London there are upwards of 300,000 inhabited houses. The whole of the evergreen branches sold number 375,000.

Even the ordinary-sized inns, I was informed, displayed holly decorations, costing from 2*s.* to 10*s.*; while in the larger inns, where, perhaps, an assembly-room, a concert-room, or a club-room, had to be adorned, along with other apartments, 20*s.* worth of holly, &c., was a not uncommon outlay. 'Well, then, consider,' said another informant, 'the plum-puddings! Why, at least there's a hundred thousand of 'em eaten, in London, through the Christmas and the month following. That's nearly one pudding to every twenty of the population, is it, sir? Well, perhaps, that's too much. But, then, there's the great numbers eaten at public dinners and suppers; and there's more plum-pudding clubs at the small grocers and public-houses than there used to be, so, say a full hundred thousand, flinging in any mince-pies that may be decorated with evergreens. Well, sir, every plum-pudding will have a sprig of holly in him. If it's bought just for the occasion, it may cost 1*d.*, to be really prime and nicely berried. If it's part of a lot, why it won't cost a halfpenny, so reckon it all at a halfpenny. What does that come to? Above 200*l*. Think of that, then, just for sprigging puddings!'

Mistletoe, I am informed, is in somewhat less demand than it was, though there might be no very perceptible difference. In many houses holly is now used instead of the true plant, for the ancient ceremonies and privileges observed 'under the mistletoe bough.' The holly is not half the price of the mistletoe, which is one reason; for, though there is not any great disparity of price, wholesale, the holly, which costs 6*d*.

Christmas Carnival, Crystal Palace 1850s

retail, is more than the quantity of mistletoe retailed for 1s. The holly-tree may be grown in any hedge, and ivy may be reared against any wall; while the mistletoe is parasitical of the apple-tree, and, but not to half the extent, of the oak and other trees. It does not grow in the northern counties of England. The purchasers of the mistletoe are, for the most part, the wealthier classes, or, at any rate, I was told, 'those who give parties.' It is bought, too, by the male servants in large establishments, and more would be so bought, 'only so few of the great people, of the most fashionable squares and places, keep their Christmas in town.' Half-a-crown is a not uncommon price for a handsome mistletoe bough.

The costermongers buy about a half of the holly, &c., brought to the markets; it is also sold either direct to those requiring evergreens, or to green-grocers and fruiterers who have received orders for it from their customers, or who know it will be wanted. A shilling's worth may be bought in the market, the bundles being divided. Mistletoe, the costers – those having regular customers in the suburbs – receive orders for. 'Last December,' said a coster to me, 'I remember a servant-girl, and she weren't such a girl either, running after me in a regular flutter, to tell me the family had forgot to order 2s. worth of mistletoe of me, to be brought next day. Oh, yes, sir, if it's ordered by, or delivered to the servant-girls, they generally have a little giggling about it. If I've said: "What are you laughing at?" they'll mostly say: "Me! I'm not laughing."' . . .

*   *   *

One strong-looking lad, of 16 or 17, gave me the following account:–

'It's hard work, is Christmasing; but, when you have neither money nor work, you must do something, and so the

holly may come in handy. I live with a elder brother; he helps the masons, and as we had neither of us either work or money, he cut off Tottenham and Edmonton way, and me the t'other side of the water, Mortlake way, as well as I know. We'd both been used to costering, off and on. I was out, I think, ten days altogether, and didn't make 6s. in it. I'd been out two Christmases before. O, yes, I'd forgot. I made 6d. over the 6s., for I had half a pork-pie and a pint of beer, and the landlord took it out in holly. I meant to have made a quarter of pork do, but I was so hungry – and so would you, sir, if you'd been out a-Christmasing – that I had the t'other quarter. It's 2d. a quarter. I did better when I was out afore, but I forget what I made. It's often slow work, for you must wait sometimes 'till no one's looking, and then you must work away like anything. I'd nothing but a sharp knife, I borrowed, and some bits of cord to tie the holly up. You *must* look out sharp, because, you see, sir, a man very likely won't like his holly-tree to be stripped. Wherever there is a berry, we goes for the berries. They're poison berries, I've heard. Moonlight nights is the thing, sir, when you knows where you are. I never goes for mizzletoe. I hardly knows it when I sees it. The first time I was out, a man got me to go for some in a orchard, and told me how to manage; but I cut my lucky in a minute. Something came over me like. I felt sickish. But what can a poor fellow do? I never lost my Christmas, but a little bit of it once. Two men took it from me, and said I ought to thank them for letting me off without a jolly good jacketing, as they was gardeners. I believes they was men out a-Christmasing, as I were. It was a dreadful cold time that; and I was wet, and hungry, – and thirsty, too, for all I was so wet, – and I'd to wait a-watching in the wet. I've got something better to do now, and I'll never go a-Christmasing again, if I can help it.'

This lad contrived to get back to his lodging, in town, every night, but some of those out Christmasing, stay two or three days and nights in the country, sleeping in barns, out-houses, carts, or under hay-stacks, inclement as the weather may be, when their funds are insufficient to defray the charge of a bed, or a part of one, at a country 'dossing-crib' (low lodging-house). They resorted, in considerable numbers, to the casual wards of the workhouses, in Croydon, Greenwich, Reigate, Dartford, &c., when that accommodation was afforded them, concealing their holly for the night.

As in other matters, it may be a surprise to some of my readers to learn in what way the evergreens, used on festive occasions in their homes, may have been procured.

The costermongers who produce their own Christmasing, generally hawk it. A few sell it by the lot to their more prosperous brethren. What the costers purchase in the market, they aim to sell at cent. per cent.

Supposing that 700 men and lads gathered their own holly, &c., and each worked for three weeks (not regarding interruptions), and calculating that, in the time they cleared even 15*s*. each, it amounts to 575*l*.

Some of the costermongers deck their carts and barrows, in the general line, with holly at Christmas. Some go out with their carts full of holly, for sale, and may be accompanied by a fiddler, or by a person beating a drum. The cry is, 'Holly! Green Holly!'

One of my informants alluded incidentally to the decoration of the churches, and I may observe that they used to be far more profusely decked with Christmas evergreens than at present; so much so, that a lady correspondent in January, 1712, complained to 'Mr. *Spectator*' that her church-going was bootless. She was constant at church, to hear divine service and make conquests; but the clerk had so overdone the greens in the church that, for three weeks, Miss Jenny Simper had not even seen the young baronet, whom she dressed for at divine

worship, although he pursued his devotions only three pews from hers. The aisle was a pretty shady walk, and each pew was an arbour. The pulpit was so clustered with holly and ivy that the congregation, like Moses, heard the word out of a bush. 'Sir Anthony Love's pew in particular,' concludes the indignant Miss Simper, 'is so well hedged, that all my batteries have no effect. I am obliged to shoot at random among the boughs without taking any manner of aim. Mr Spectator, unless you'll give orders for removing these greens, I shall grow a very awkward creature at church, and soon have little else to do there but to say my prayers.' In a subsquent number, the clerk glorifies himself that he had checked the ogling of Miss Simper. He had heard how the Kentish men evaded the Conqueror by displaying green boughs before them, and so he bethought him of a like device against the love-warfare of this coquettish lady.

The Forbidden Child

LEON GARFIELD

Children's writer Leon Garfield was brought up in Brighton but would often spend Christmas in London with his Jewish aunts and uncles. This short story vividly

· *A London Christmas* ·

portrays the intense feelings of a young Jewish boy as he longs passionately to be included in festivities forbidden to him by his religion.

The pleasures of youth are best remembered; those of age are best savoured as they come. So it is with Christmases. Best to forget the awful certainty that the world would end on December 24; or that for some equally cogent reason Christmas would never come, so that, when it did come, one was so over-wrought with anxiety on its behalf that one was infallibly sick and infallibly given castor oil.

Best to remember Victoria Station, where my Christmases always seemed to begin. A magical hissing cave of steam and tinsel bazaars, with nuts, grapes and oranges piled high in the fruit-shop window, like gorgeous Alps under eternal cotton wool; and herald angels singing under the clock and shaking scarlet collecting boxes. Best to remember the bus – or, if times were good, a taxi smelling like a wallet – to an Aunt and Uncle grand in North London, with a river at the bottom of their garden and a statue of Samson modestly endeavouring to thrust aside the pillars of a rustic arch.

Best to forget that other Aunt and Uncle (mortal enemies of the first), to whom I was sometimes despatched, and who lived in tomb-like seclusion in Highbury New Park. Charity bids me to think better of them now than I did at the time. (But Charity! you weren't there!) Fancy suggests that there had once been a Christmas in that tall glum house, and that there had been holly; but its berries got frightened white and turned into the moth-balls on which I always trod when I crept out of bed in the middle of the night.

Although I was Jewish all the year round, I never really felt it till I got into that house, where the very name, Jesus, was not to be pronounced, and the New Testament was a Satanic text. My Aunt and Uncle hated Christmas and, what was

worse, denied its very existence, which angered me very much as I knew it was happening at Selfridges, on the top floor. Jesus was there, very small and pink, sitting with his proud mother in a cave of holly and sand; and so was Father Christmas, in a boat. You reached this enchanted place by means of a lift, straight out of the Arabian Nights, that was operated by a lady in pale blue velvet, with beauty spots and a powdered wig. She resembled something between a female dragoon and Marie Antoinette, and had the most refined voice I have ever heard. When she said: 'Going up!' it was just my soul that soared, for all earthly parts were left behind.

Father Christmas in Harrod's Toy Department

But of course I never went to Selfridges on those Christmases when I stayed in Highbury New Park; where I seem to remember that the curtains were always drawn, in case some hint of pagan festivity might sparkle through. Looking back on it, I must have presented a very doleful, piteous sight, imprisoned with that gloomy pair, while the world sang outside. My Uncle was a large-faced, shouting man of whom I lived in mortal terror. My Aunt, on first acquaintance, was short. She had a round face and currant eyes, like a bun; but I soon discovered it was a bun on which a tiger might well have broken its teeth. (But Charity bids me think better of them now!)

They had a garden, but no river and no Samson. It was a condemned patch of grass imprisoned by a wall on which was a thick crust of broken glass. You got to it by an iron staircase, such as prisons have. These, then, were the Christmases it is best to forget. And yet, there is one that I remember . . .

There was a woman who came to clean, a Mrs Blowser, who had been worn down over the years into something faint and shadowy in a flowered overall. No spark of joy or pleasure ever came off her; in fact, she was ideally suited to Highbury New Park. She never spoke to me, never smiled, and came and went like a ghost. She would come on Christmas Eve, and, before she left, would murmur to my Aunt (as if something unavoidable had occurred at home), that she wouldn't be coming for the next two days. No reason was given, and none was asked. My Aunt knew perfectly well that Christmas was to blame; but no word of it was ever mentioned.

I don't know whether Mrs Blowser ever nursed a sense of grievance; possibly she did. At all events, on this particular Christmas Eve, after she'd made her mysterious communication, she stared drearily at me and then said to my Aunt that she'd 'take him off her hands for the afternoon, if that would be all right, ma'am'. 'Where to?' asked my Aunt. 'To the park,' said Mrs Blowser, with a sense of wretchedness altogether fitting. I knew that park. It was all railings and stern keepers, and half a dozen depressed rabbits behind bars. 'Very well,' said my Aunt, detecting no possible source of joyfulness in the plan.

I went with Mrs Blowser and we walked silently in the park for about half an hour; and then she said, fainting with distress: 'I thought we might call on my sister-in-law what lives quite near.' I said it sounded an agreeable idea, so we walked to a street of small terraced houses with dust-bins and bottles outside.

Mrs Blowser's sister-in-law's house was Number Fourteen. It was tiny – no bigger than a doll's house, it seemed to me. The ceilings were low, the walls close together, and the fireplace was of the waistcoat pocket variety, and stuffed full of fire. Mrs B's sister-in-law's house was full of children and toys and noise and the steamy smell of puddings and mince pies; it was full of candles and coloured lights and shining faces. Mrs B's sister-in-law was giving a Christmas Party. 'I've brought him,' said Mrs Blowser, dolefully, 'Poor little soul!'

Never can I remember a Christmas like it. Never can I remember such mountains of food and such shrieking, thumping, banging and happy games! There was Charades, and Hunt the Thimble, and Blind Man's Buff and Postman's Knock. Oh how I remember an angelic girl who smelt of burnt sugar and came blushing out for a kiss when I knocked! There was a lighted tree and a snow-storm of cards and a Christmas Crib on the sideboard. Long I gazed at it; long I gazed at the Forbidden Child, lying in a match-box, in white crepe swaddling bands, tied with a tinsel sash. And there were the Three Wise Men, travelling on horseback from the direction of a family photograph. I think they were Red Indians in private life; but were attired for the occasion in flowing Arab robes.

'I'll have to be taking him back, now,' said Mrs B after what

had seemed like scarcely five minutes. 'Can we give him a present?' inquired the sister-in-law. (My heart rose.) 'They wouldn't like it,' said Mrs B. (My heart sank.) 'Something small?' suggested the sister-in-law. 'If he don't say nothing about it,' said Mrs B. 'I know what!' said the sister-in-law. 'I'll give him this. He's had his eye on it ever since he come in.' She went to the Crib and gave me the matchbox with the Forbidden Child. 'I got another one upstairs.'

Never will I forget my guilty delight as I walked back to Highbury New Park with Mrs B. 'You won't say nothing to 'em,' she said. I shook my head. 'I'll catch it if you let on.' I nodded. 'What will you tell 'em then if they asks?' I pondered. 'I'll think of something,' I said.

My Aunt and Uncle were waiting. 'You've been a long time, Mrs Blowser.' 'We called at my sister-in-law's, ma'am,' said Mrs Blowser. 'For a cup of tea.'

After Mrs B had gone, my Aunt remarked that I looked flushed and that there were crumbs round my mouth; cake crumbs. 'They were having a party,' I mumbled, feeling it useless to deny that much. 'Party? What sort of party?' demanded my Uncle in a most menacing fashion. 'A birthday party,' I said. 'Whose birthday?' my Uncle inquired even more menacingly. 'A baby's, Uncle.' 'What? A party for a baby? I never heard of such a thing!' 'Really, Uncle, it was! On my word of honour!' And then I added, with a burst of inspiration: 'It was a Jewish baby, Uncle. On my word of honour, it was!'

from

The Diaries of
John Evelyn

*In the seventeenth century the puritans condemned not only
the pagan but the Christian origins of Christmas because
of their Popish antecedents and because, as the main
national holiday, it had become a time for drinking,
dancing and gambling. Indeed in 1652 they even
attempted to abolish Christmas, forbidding the Prayer
Book service for Christmas Day. The Act of Parliament
read: 'No observation shall be had of the five-and-
twentieth day of December, commonly called Christmas
Day; nor any solemnity used or exercised in churches upon
the day in respect thereof.' Some extremists attacked
Christmas Day as 'the old Heathen's Feasting Day, in
honour to Saturn their Idol-God'. And so, for about eight
years there were no official Christmas masses or celebrations.*

*John Evelyn – a strong Royalist and pious Anglican –
defied the authorities by attending the illegal Prayer Book
services held in London in the 1650s. From 1652 to
1655 he notes in his diary the absence of services in
London, though in 1652 he discovered an 'honest' divine
who preached at Lewisham on Boxing Day; and in 1656*

· A London Christmas ·

*he travelled to London specially to receive the sacrament at
'Dr Wild's lodgings, where I rejoiced to find so full an
assembly of devout and sober Christians.' The following
extract is his account of what happened on Christmas
Day, 1657, when he was arrested along with the whole
congregation worshipping privately at Exeter Chapel,
West of Temple Bar, as they were receiving Holy
Communion.*

I went with my Wife &c: to *Lond*: to celebrate *Christmas day*. Mr
Gunning preaching in *Exesceter* Chapell on 7. *Micha* 2. Sermon
Ended, as he was giving us the holy Sacrement, The Chapell was
surrounded with Soldiers: All the Communicants and Assembly
surpriz'd & kept Prisoners by them, some in the house, others
carried away: It fell to my share to be confined to a roome in the
house, where yet were permitted to Dine with the master of it,
the Countesse of *Dorset, Lady Hatton* &c some others of quality
who invited me: In the afternoone came *Collonel Whalley*, Goffe
& others from *Whitehall* to examine us one by one, & some they
committed to the *Martial*, some to Prison, some Committed:
When I came before them they tooke my name and aboad,
examined me, why contrarie to an Ordinance made that none
should any longer observe the superstitious time of the Nativity
(so esteem'd by them) I durst offend, & particularly be at
Common prayers, which they told me was but the *Masse in
English*, & particularly pray for *Charles* stuard, for which we had
no scripture: I told them we did not pray for *Cha: Steward* but for
all *Christian Kings, Princes and Governors:* They replied, in so
doing we praied for the K. of *Spaine* too, who was their enemie,
& a *Papist*, with other frivolous & insnaring questions, with
much threatning, & finding no colour to detaine me longer,
with much pitty of my Ignorance, they dismiss'd me: These
men were of high flight, and above Ordinances: & spake spiteful
things of our B. Lord nativity.

from

Child's Parties: And A Remonstrance Concerning Them

WILLIAM THACKERAY

This first appeared in Punch *as part of the 'Snob Papers'
– a series of articles which made Thackeray famous.
Children's parties were still a novelty in the mid-
nineteenth century and Thackeray's first step in remedying
the evil is to lay some of the responsibility on Mr Punch,
whose illustrator John Leech whitewashes the children's
ball by portraying it as some kind of paradise.*

Sir, – As your publication finds its way to almost every
drawing-room table in this metropolis, and is read by the
young and old in every family, I beseech you to give admission
to the remonstrance of an unhappy parent, and to endeavour to
put a stop to a practice which appears to me to be increasing

Christmas Card printed in London by Marcus Wood, 1890s

daily, and is likely to operate most injuriously upon the health, morals, and comfort of society in general.

The awful spread of Juvenile Parties, sir, is the fact to which I would draw your attention. There is no end to those entertainments, and if the custom be not speedily checked, people will be obliged to fly from London at Christmas, and hide their children during the holidays. I gave mine warning in a speech at breakfast this day, and said with tears in my eyes that if the Juvenile Party system went on, I would take a house at Margate next winter, for that, by heavens! I could not bear another Juvenile Season in London.

If they would but transfer Innocents' Day to the summer holidays, and let the children have their pleasures in May or June, we might get on. But now in this most ruthless and cut-throat season of sleet, thaw, frost, wind, snow, mud, and sore throats, it is quite a tempting of fate to be going much abroad; and this is the time of all others that is selected for the amusement of our little darlings.

As the first step towards the remedying of the evil of which I complain, I am obliged to look *Mr Punch* himself in his venerable beard, and say, 'You sir, have, by your agents, caused not a little of the mischief'. I desire that, during Christmas time at least, Mr Leech should be abolished, or sent to take a holiday. Judging from his sketches, I should say that he must be endowed with a perfectly monstrous organ of philoprogenitiveness; he revels in the delineation of the dearest and most beautiful little boys and girls in turn-down collars and broad sashes, and produces in your *Almanack* a picture of a child's costume ball, in which he has made the little wretches in the dresses of every age, and looking so happy, beautiful, and charming, that I have carefully kept the picture from the sight of the women and children of my own household, and – I will not say burned it, for I had not the heart to do that – but locked it away privately, lest they should conspire to have a costume ball themselves, and little Polly should insist upon appearing in the dress of Anne Boleyne, or little Jacky upon turning out as an Ancient Briton.

An odious, revolting and disagreeable practice sir, I say, ought not to be described in a manner so atrociously pleasing. The real satirist has no right to lead the public astray about the Juvenile *Fête* nuisance, and to describe a child's ball as if it was a sort of Paradise, and the little imps engaged as happy and pretty as so many cherubs. They should be drawn, one and all, as hideous – disagreeable – distorted – affected – jealous of each other – dancing awkwardly – with shoes too tight for them – over-eating themselves at supper – very unwell (and deservedly so) the next morning, with Mamma administering a mixture made after the Doctor's prescription, and which should be painted awfully black, in an immense large teacup, and (as might be shown by the horrible expression on the little patient's face) of the most disgusting flavour. Banish, I say, that Mr Leech during Christmas time, at least; for, by a misplaced kindness and absurd fondness for children, he is likely to do them and their parents an incalculable quantity of harm.

As every man, sir, looks at the world out of his own eyes or spectacles, or, in other words, speaks of it as he finds it himself, I will lay before you my own case, being perfectly sure that many another parent will sympathize with me. My family, already inconveniently large, is yet constantly on the increase, and it is out of the question that Mrs Spec [A name sometimes assumed by the writer in his contributions to *Punch*] should go to parties, as that admirable woman has the best of occupations at home; where she is always nursing the baby. Hence it becomes the father's duty to accompany his children abroad, and to give them pleasure during the holidays.

Our own place of residence is in South Carolina Place, Clapham Road North, in one of the most healthy of the suburbs of this great City. But our relatives and acquaintances are numerous; and they are spread all over the town and its outskirts. Mrs S. has sisters married, and dwelling respectively in Islington, Haverstock Hill, Bedford Place, Upper Baker Street, and Tyburn Gardens; besides the children's grandmother, Kensington Gravel Pits, whose parties we are all of course obliged to attend. A *very* great connexion of ours, and *nearly related* to a B-r-n-t and MP, lives not a hundred miles from B-lg-ve Square. I could enumerate a dozen more places where our kinsmen or intimate friends are – heads of families every one of them, with their quivers more or less full of little arrows.

What is the consequence? I herewith send it to you in the shape of these eighteen enclosed notes, written in various styles more or less correct and corrected, from Miss Fanny's,

The Children's Party

aged seven, who hopes in round hand, that her dear cousins will come and drink tea with her on New Year's Eve, her birthday, – to that of the Governess of the B-r-n-t in question, who requests the pleasure of our company at a ball, a conjuror, and a Christmas Tree. Mrs Spec, for the valid reason above stated, cannot frequent these meetings: I am the deplorable chaperon of the young people. I am called upon to conduct my family five miles to tea at six o'clock. No count is taken of our personal habits, hours of dinner, or intervals of rest. We are made the victims of an infantile conspiracy, nor will the lady of the house hear of any revolt or denial.

'Why,' says she, with the spirit which becomes a woman and mother, 'you go to your *man's* parties eagerly enough: what an unnatural wretch you must be to grudge your children their pleasures!' She looks round, sweeps all six of them into her arms, whilst the baby on her lap begins to bawl, and you are assailed by seven pairs of imploring eyes, against which there is no appeal. You must go. If you are dying of lumbago, if you are engaged to the best of dinners, if you are longing to stop at home and read Macaulay, you must give up all and go.

And it is not to one Party or two, but to almost all. You must go to the Gravel Pits, otherwise the grandmother will cut the children out of her will, and leave her property to her *other* grandchildren. If you refuse Islington, and accept Tyburn Gardens, you sneer at a poor relation, and acknowledge a rich one readily enough. If you decline Tyburn Gardens, you fling away the chances of the poor dear children in life, and the hopes of the cadetship for little Jacky. If you go to Hampstead, having declined Bedford Place, it is because you never refuse an invitation to Hampstead, where they make much of you, and Miss Maria is pretty, (as *you* think, though your wife doesn't,) and do not care for the Doctor in Bedford Place. And if you accept Bedford Place, you dare not refuse Upper Baker Street, because there is a coolness between the two families, and you must on no account seem to take part with one or the other.

In this way many a man besides myself, I dare say, finds himself miserably tied down, and a helpless prisoner, like Gulliver in the hands of the Lilliputians. Let us just enumerate a few of the miseries of the pitiable parental slave.

In the first place, examine the question in a pecuniary point of view. The expenses of children's toilets at this present time are perfectly frightful.

My eldest boy, Gustavus, at home from Dr Birch's Academy, Rodwell Regis, wears turquoise studs, fine linen shirts, white waist-coats, and shiny boots: and, when I proposed that he should go to a party in Berlin gloves, asked me if I wished that he should be mistaken for a footman? My second, Augustus, grumbles about getting his elder brother's clothes, nor could he be brought to accommodate himself to Gustavus's waistcoats at all, had not his mother coaxed him by the loan of her chain and watch, which latter the child broke after many desperate attempts to wind it up. As for the little fellow, Adolphus, his mother has him attired in a costume partly Scotch, partly Hungarian, mostly buttons, and with a Louis Quatorze hat and scarlet feather, and she curls this child's hair with her own blessed tongs every night.

I wish she would do as much for the girls, though: but no, Monsieur Floridor must do that: and accordingly, every day this season, that abominable little Frenchman, who is, I have no doubt, a Red Republican, and smells of cigars and hair-oil, comes over, and, at a cost of eighteenpence *par tête*, figs out my little creatures' heads with fixature, bandoline, crinoline – the deuce knows what.

The bill for silk stockings, sashes, white frocks, is so enormous, that I have not been able to pay my own tailor these three years.

The bill for flys to 'Amstid and back, to Hizzlington and take up, &c., is fearful. The drivers, in this extra weather, must be paid extra, and they drink extra. Having to go to Hackney in the snow, on the night of the 5th of January, our man was so hopelessly inebriated, that I was compelled to get out and drive myself; and I am now, on what is called Twelfth Day (with, of course, another child's party before me for the evening), writing this from my bed, sir, with a severe cold, a violent toothache, and a most acute rheumatism.

As I hear the knock of our medical man, whom an anxious

wife has called in, I close this letter; asking leave, however, if I survive, to return to this painful subject next week. And, wishing you a *merry!* New Year, I have the honour to be, dear *Mr Punch*,

Your constant reader,
SPEC.

The Metropolitan Police at Christmas

Although Christmas is a holiday for most people, the police are always kept busy at this time of the year having to deal with an increasing number of accidents and criminal offences. The following reports from London newspapers span a period of over a hundred years.

The Gentleman's Magazine, 1822

Charles Clapp, Benjamin Jackson, Denis Jelks, and Robert Prinset, were brought to Bow Street Office by O. Bond, the constable, charged with performing on several musical instruments in St Martin's Lane, at half-past twelve o'clock on Christmas morning, by Mr Munroe, the authorised principal Wait, appointed by the Court of Burgesses for the City and Liberty of Westminster, who alone considers himself entitled,

by his appointment, to apply for Christmas Boxes. He also urged that the prisoners, acting as minstrels, came under the meaning of the Vagrant Act, alluded to in 17th Geo. II.; however, on reference to the last Vagrant Act of the present King, the word 'minstrels' is omitted; consequently they are no longer cognizable under that Act of Parliament; and in addition to that, Mr Charles Clapp, one of the prisoners, produced his indenture of having served seven years as an apprentice to the profession of a musician to Mr Clay, who held the same appointment as Mr Munroe does under the Court of Burgesses. The prisoners were discharged, after receiving an admonition from Mr Hall, the sitting magistrate, not to collect Christmas Boxes.

The London Illustrated News, **1850**

Skating in the Parks: Though the ice was but very thin on Sunday last, the number of skaters in all the parks was very great, and there were numerous immersions. One of a fatal character occurred in the Serpentine where a respectably attired young man, who was skating on the South side, near the aqueduct, broke in, and became immersed in twelve feet of water. Superintendent Murphy and iceman Deze immediately proceeded to his assistance but he was quite dead. The body was conveyed to the Royal Humane Society's receiving-house, where prompt remedies were applied by the surgeons, but, unfortunately, without effect. The body was then removed by the parochial authorities to await the inquest, and also to be owned. The name of the deceased was Thomas Drayton, and was in the employ of Messrs, Chalton & Easton, tea-dealers, Charing-cross.

A London Newspaper, Dec. 1927

The members of the 'Silver Slipper' Club continued their revels into Christmas morning. . . . No regard to season is paid in

police procedure. Christmas morning in the police is the same as any other morning. Therefore arrangements were made for inspecting the 'Silver Slipper' on Christmas morning. The police were satisfied to take the names and addresses of those present together with bottled samples.

from

In Pleasant Places

JOYCE GRENFELL

For a child brought up in the city, spending Christmas away from home in unfamiliar surroundings can make the occasion particularly magical. Joyce Grenfell was born and educated in London in the early part of this century, but like many upper-middle class children she would leave the capital during the winter holidays to spend Christmas with relations in the country.

On the whole I enjoy preparing for events more than the event itself. The idea of Christmas always fired me, and even as a child it was the getting-ready period I liked most – making presents and cards, gumming coloured paper rings together for chains, and posting my personal list of requests up the chimney to Father Christmas.

· A London Christmas ·

The feast itself was always, from as far back as my memory goes, spent staying at Cliveden with Aunt Nancy and Uncle Waldorf Astor and their five children. My ambivalent feelings about the place exercised me a good deal. I was torn between wishing we could have our own family Christmas at home – decorating our own tree, putting up our own holly and mistletoe – and the greedy certainty that at the big house there would be lots more people, presents, festivity and foods. As the day drew nearer I settled for greed and hoped there wouldn't be a family row and that pleasures would be plentiful.

We usually arrived on Christmas Eve in the dark at tea-time, the car sent to fetch us from Taplow Station loaded with our baggage and the parcels Tommy and I were not supposed to notice. 'Mummy, what's in that?' 'Wait and see – it's Christmas.' As we turned the corner by the giant marble shell fountain, at the end of the straight quarter-mile approach to the house, the glassed-in porch as if by magic suddenly blazed with light. How did anyone know we were coming? I only discovered years later than when a car passed through the main iron gates of the park the lodge-keeper telephoned, on a hand-wound private line, to warn the house that it was coming. The butler was at the open door to greet us. 'Shake hands with Mr Lee.' We did and said we were quite well, thank you, to him and to the footmen waiting to carry in the bags. We shook hands, too, with the parlourmaid, hovering behind them, in her dark brown alpaca uniform with a gossamer-fine organdie apron, high collar, and head bandeau cap tied with brown velvet ribbon.

We sniffed the special Cliveden smell as we stepped into the porch, where, as well as tennis racquets, hockey-sticks and golf-bags, there was a giant Chinese jar, full of golf-umbrellas, walking-sticks and a special 'pusher' – a polished wooden device, like a wide, shallow, spread-out crutch – which legend said had been designed to fit the waist of some elderly, stout party, to push her up the long and steep yew-tree walk that rises up to the house from the riverside below. It had been sold with the house when old Mr Astor bought it from the Duke of Westminster. We took it in turns to push each other up and down the front hall with it, until some grown-up stopped us. The delicious smell came from pots of humea; a delicate plant with a feathery cascade of reddish-brown flowers that give off an incense-like scent; not much to look at, but lovely to sniff. (It is increasingly hard to buy humea. A year or two ago Reggie discovered that one of the few places where it is grown is in the commercial nursery garden at Windsor Castle. He managed to get hold of a pot, and for about ten days the flat was heady with its scent.)

In the front hall we saw the giant Christmas tree was where we expected it to be, at the foot of the oak staircase. The banisters were festooned with garlands of box, yew, bay, ivy, holly and other evergreens that, as well as the humea, gave off a subtle aromatic scent. Only once were we allowed to help decorate the tree. The job was usually done by a gardener on a step-ladder, with the housekeeper handing him the tinsel and coloured balls. I always made sure that certain favourite decorations were still there; the glass birds in little tin cages were regulars I looked for.

Aunt Nancy, wearing a sweater over a silk shirt, neat tweed skirt, golf socks and ghillie shoes, came out of her boudoir to greet us.

'You children go on upstairs – and take your coats with you. I will not have them left all over the place.' She was rather fierce, and, after kissing her proffered cheek and feeling, as always, as if I had done something wrong, I scrambled up the polished stairs.

'Come on down right away as soon as you have washed. You needn't change today. Tea's ready.'

· A London Christmas ·

Ordinarily we always 'changed' for tea. As little girls my cousin Wissie and I (the only girls of the party until our Brand cousins, Virginia and Dinah, were old enough to come for Christmas) put on frilly muslins and our bronze dancing-slippers with elastic that crossed our ankles. As we grew older we graduated to velvet and fine wool. The boys began in their sailor suits, but once they were old enough to go to school they wore the small boys' uniform of grey flannel jacket and shorts with black elastic-sided 'house-shoes'.

We came down and sat at the children's table near the fire, where Uncle Waldorf chose to join us. He poured out our milk and sliced the wholesome loaf and plain cake baked for us to eat. At the grown-up table, where Aunt Nancy presided, there were delectable little scones in a lidded silver dish, kept hot over a spirit lamp. There was also a special, almost black, rich fruit-cake topped with marzipan, chocolate éclairs and very short crisp shortbreads, all made in the still-room by two full-time cake-and-pastry-cooks. Sometimes we were allowed special treats from the grown-ups' table, but Aunt Nancy kept an eye on the goodies, and we were strictly rationed.

After tea Aunt Nancy went to her present-room, a small dark panelled study next to her boudoir used for storage. No child was allowed to go there, particularly at Christmas-time, but, once when I was about sixteen and was sent in there to fetch something for her, I saw it was like a little shop. Piles of sweaters of all colours and sizes, men's, boys', women's and girls'; silk stockings, silk scarves, chiffon squares and boxes of linen handkerchiefs, from the Irish Linen Stores, initialled for everyone in the party. There were evening bags, men's ties, golf-balls in boxes, little packs of tees, diaries, toys, games, books and candy. *Lots* of candy. There was never a more generous present-giver than Aunt Nancy, but she was always careful about her candy store; most of it came from American friends, and she didn't let it out of her keeping except in very

Illustrated London News Christmas Number 1890s

occasional bestowals of a caramel here and a sour-ball there. She also had a great many boxes of chewing-gum and was never without a supply in her pocket. Presents from the store were given to everyone in the house, family, friends, staff and visiting staff – in those days ladies' maids and valets always accompanied their employers. Aunt Nancy's private secretary helped by doing much of the present buying, and all the wrapping up in layers of best quality tissue-paper tied with inch-wide red satin ribbon. Aunt Nancy wrote the tags.

At about half-past six the bell-ringers and carol-singers, steaming a little from the outside damp and exercise, arrived in the hall. I thought of the bell-ringers as old men, but I don't suppose they can have been, as they had walked all the way from Burnham to play for us. We were all summoned to hear them. Each man had two bells, and they stood in pairs facing each other. At a nod from their leader they began to ring. First they rang *The Blue Bells of Scotland*, a tradition of their visit and not the most Christmassy of choices. They didn't just play it once – they played it again, and again, and again. The bells were very loud. And then it was time for the carol-singers. All I remember is a small group of men and boys in dark clothes; one hooty tenor who, before the group joined in, swooped through an opening solo verse of *See Amid the Winter Snows* with all the notes run together. This, for some reason, gave me bad church-giggles. Wissie caught it. The boys became infected, too. Aunt Nancy gave us fierce frowns. It happened every year. I half-hoped, half-dreaded the swooper would swoop again; and every year he did.

After the carols we were sent upstairs to bed, and on our way we stopped at Uncle Waldorf's dressing-room, where his valet had put out a selection of stockings for us to choose from, in anticipation of Father Christmas's visit later that night. My father was a non-sporting Londoner who neither played golf nor shot. His short City socks were no good for hanging up;

Uncle Waldorf's beautifully hand-knitted knee-length stockings were ideal. As very small children we didn't open our stockings until we took them to our parents' room, and there in their bed we discovered what it was that crackled and tinkled and bulged so enchantingly. As we grew older we opened them in our own beds at whatever hour we woke up and felt the precious weight, and heard the sounds a really good stocking can make. Nursery breakfast was upstairs. After giving us all time to go to the bathroom and 'be good', and after waiting for our parents to finish their breakfast in the dining-room, we were allowed to go downstairs.

Goose Clubs

In the nineteenth century lotteries and clubs sprang up all over the country, for the first time ensuring that even artisans on a very meagre wage were able to purchase a traditional Christmas dinner. In London practically every third-rate inn and back-street public house was the centre for a Plum Pudding or Goose Club, the announcement of which would stare you in the face twenty times in the course of a day's walk, usually with the guarantee that this club was 'all fair and proper and above board'. Although beef stayed popular in the north, in London goose became the chosen Christmas meat. This was because it was cheaper to buy, being both tougher than beef or turkey and easier to transport *en masse*.

To obtain his goose the working man paid a small weekly

The Goose Club drawn by Phiz from the *Illustrated London News*, 24 December 1853

sum from his wages for the thirteen weeks leading up to Christmas (if the amount came to more than the cost of the goose, then a bottle or two of spirits were thrown in). On Christmas Eve subscribers assembled in the lottery room of the local public house. The walls were hung with holly and evergreen while the assortments of bird and bottle, with labels attached, were arranged around the room. Corresponding tickets were put in a hat and each subscriber would then pull out one which guaranteed him the portion indicated by his lot.

The landlord usually divided and classified the prizes. This was considered a fairer method than that of simply throwing a die and letting each man choose for himself, since most men wouldn't have been able to tell which were the prize birds. The club was therefore a kind of lottery with some people fairing much better than others. In London, there was at least a bird –

no matter how scrawny – for every subscriber; in the country some received nothing.

Opinion at the time varied as to the merits of such clubs. Charles Manby Smith, writing in 1853 when the clubs were at the height of their popularity, saw them as worthy institutions that had been established in response to the needs and wants of the labouring classes. He believed that having to give up six pence a week to the 'Christmas bank' tamed the moneyless classes in their drinking habits, since they soon found they could do quite as much work with one pot of beer a day as they could with two. In this way not only could they learn prudence, but also were able to provide their family with a plum pudding and goose for Christmas. The following extract from *Curiosities of London Life* by Manby Smith extolls the virtues of these clubs.

Unfashionable Clubs

We know nothing of the original genius who first hit upon this mode of indoctrinating the lower orders in a way so much to their advantage; we hope, however, as there is little reason to doubt, that he found his own account in it, and reaped his well-deserved reward. Whoever he was, his example has been well followed for many years past. In the poorer and more populous districts of the metropolis, this practice of making provision for inevitable wants, by small subscriptions paid in advance, prevails to a large extent. As winter sets in, almost every provision-dealer, and other traders as well, proffers a compact to the public, which he calls a club, though it is more of the nature of a savings-bank, seeing that, at the expiration of the subscribing period, every member is a creditor of the shop to the amount of his own investments, and nothing more. Thus, besides the Plum-pudding Clubs, there are Coal Clubs, by which the poor man who invests 1s. a week for five or six of the summer months, gets a ton of good coal laid in for the winter's consumption before the frost sets in and the coal becomes dear. Then there is the Goose Club, which the wiser members manage among themselves by contracting with a country dealer, and thus avoid the tipsy consummation of the public-house, where these clubs have mostly taken shelter. Again, there is the Twelfth-cake Club, which comes to a head soon after Christmas, and is more of a lottery than a club, inasmuch as the large cakes are raffled for, and the losers, if they get anything, get but a big bun for their pains and penalties. All these clubs, it will be observed, are plants of winter-growth, or at least of winter-fruiting, having for their object the provision of something desirable or indispensable in the winter season.

But being associated with drinking gave these clubs a bad reputation, especially with the temperance movement. The *Illustrated London News*, on Christmas Eve 1853, criticized such clubs for encouraging men to drink, because it was expected that when the men came to pay their instalments they would have a drop of their favourite liquor before departing. 'It is', declared the magazine, 'the drunkard's joy or the tippler's excuse and frequently the sober and honest man's cup of enlistment' – resulting all too often in death or the ruin of a family, it was claimed.

My Sister and Myself

J.R. ACKERLEY

The sheer extravagance of Christmas and the abundance of produce displayed in shops has always been offensive and distasteful to some people. In 1952 J.R. Ackerley, writer and literary editor of The Listener *between 1935 and 1959, recalled this in his diary.*

The Movietone News this week had a Christmas feature. A large number of flustered turkeys were driven towards the camera, and the commentator remarked that the Christmas rush was on, or words to that effect. Next they were seen crowded about their feeding trough, making their gobbling turkey fuss, and the commentator observed, with dry humour (again I do not remember his exact words), that it was no use their holding a protest meeting, for they were for it in the morning. Similar facetious jokes followed them wherever they went, hurrying and trampling about in their silly way; for to make them look as silly as possible was no doubt part of the joke and easy to achieve: turkeys, like hens, like all animals, are beautiful in themselves, and have even a kind of dignity

Father Christmas with horses

when they are leading their own lives, but the fowls, in particular, look foolish when they are being frightened.

These jolly, lip-licking sallies, delivered in the rich, cultivated, self-confident voice of one who has no sort of doubt of his own superiority to the animal kingdom, raised no laugh from the considerable audience, I was pleased to note. I took it from the silence that many other people besides myself would have been glad to be spared jeers and jibes at these creatures who, parting unwillingly with their lives, were to afford us pleasure at our Christmas tables. It reminded me of a shop window I noticed in Marylebone High Street, not many weeks ago. A whole calf's head was displayed upon a dish, and the tongue of the dead thing had been dragged out and twisted round into the side of its mouth so that it appeared, idiotically, to be licking its own lips over the taste of its own dead flesh. In order to make it more foolish still, a tomato had been balanced on top of its head. How arrogant people are in their behaviour to the domestic beasts at least. Indeed, yes, we feed upon them and enjoy their flesh; but does that permit us to make fun of them before they die or after they are dead? If it were possible, without disordering one's whole life, to be a vegetarian, I would be one; nothing could have been more disgusting and degrading than the insensitiveness displayed by these two exhibitions I have described.

from

Old Soho Days and Other Memories

THE MOTHER KATE

The Mother Kate ran St Saviour's Priory in Hackney during the early part of this century. She was part of the great benevolent movement that swept the country in the mid-Victorian period. With over a thousand charities in London alone by the turn of the century, Christmas was a time when even the very poorest could expect to have a decent

meal. As the season became increasingly commercial vagrants and unemployed men would head towards London in order to find casual labour in the weeks leading up to Christmas.

Mother Kate's priory stood next to the 'Kip', which was a men's lodging-house, described by the author as 'superior in respectability and morals to many East End lodging-houses' and frequented by men commonly classified in the neighbourhood as 'mumpers', but who were 'very harmless, and quite amenable to order'. The following extract is from a chapter headed 'Christmas Day in the "Kip", 1904'.

The caretaker at the men's lodging-house, or 'Kip,' as it is called, had been making each of the men put by a penny a week out of their earnings, and had put by his own little bit too, so that the 'Missis' was able to get them a real good dinner on Christmas Day. This was the news the Sister heard one day, and two of us settled to join the festive party. The day itself was an exceptionally beautiful one – not too cold, no rain, plenty of sunshine, and dry under foot. It even seemed to brighten up poor gray old Haggerston; and it was nice in the early morning to see the crowds of people pouring out of the churches after the early celebrations: as the six o'clock communicants trooped out, the seven o'clock crowded in, and these were succeeded again by the eight o'clock ones. A good many of the dear 'Mrs Fridays' went to the eight o'clock service at St Mary's, and behaved with the greatest reverence, although, of course, they did not make their communions. The morning wore away, and three o'clock was the hour when the feast was to begin, so about that time the caretaker's Missis, white-aproned and smiling, was seen to rush into the street from the lodging-house, capture a small boy, and send him across to the Priory to tell us 'dinner was ready to be dished up.' Off we

The first known Christmas card commissioned by Sir Henry
Cole, 1843

went, up the two newly-whitened doorsteps, along the narrow
passage, and down the dark and tortuous stairs into the
kitchen. Here a splendid fire was glowing in scarlet depths
behind the bars of the grate – a large grate it was – so arranged
that the men could on ordinary days each cook his own little
particular 'relish,' whether it was a bloater or a kipper, or
whatever might be the fancy of the moment. Two tables ran
down the room, where the poor fellows – these failures of
society, out at elbow, out of heart, out of pocket, out of
friends, and very often out of work – were seated round in
pleased expectancy. Most of them were old and worn and bent,
and life's troubles had left traces on all their countenances;
some were younger, one was a lad, and two were quite boys;
but all were ill-clad, unkempt, and dirty.

In the back kitchen the caretaker was carving meat as hard as he could, while an assistant scooped up mealy potatoes and succulent vegetables out of attendant pots, and heaped them on to the plates, the whole making a sort of delicious harmony of red, white, and green. The Missis handed the plates to the company, saying, 'Here you are: are you all served? Them as has got knives and forks use them, and them as ain't must eat with their fingers.' In due course of time they were all served; one young, rather impudent-looking man, called out, 'Say, how do I look behind all this?' pointing to the tri-coloured heap on his plate. One poor old man, wrinkled, worn, and bent, looked sadly at the plate before him, as he gently adjusted the potato with the tip of his finger so that it soaked up more gravy. He was one of the knife-and-forkless ones. Jars of salt, cups of mustard, and saucers of pickles were scattered over the table. But before the fray began, the Missis shouted out, 'Now then, stand up every one of you, and Sister'll say grace.' Sister did, and the voice of an old man from the remote depths of the corner called out, 'Thank ye kindly, mum, the same to you, and many on 'em.' And then they began to attack the food. It was like Prince Charlie's Highlanders at Culloden, those who had weapons used them, those who hadn't used their fingers. We found they were not all assembled though. Wavering and uncertain steps descended the stairs, and gentlemen who had evidently been 'refreshing' to a slight extent, stumbled in, very eager to shake hands with the Sisters, and very loth to leave go each Sister's hand when shaken. But the Missis sent them to their places, and ordered them to eat. A blear-eyed puppy, who was sitting in the fender, thought it a good opportunity to crawl out and wander under the table, hopeful of bits, also two kittens, but they, bolder and more capable than the puppy, climbed up the men's legs, and so brought themselves on a level with the table. Cages of poor little cramped birds hung on the walls, and they sung and chirped and twittered as if they wished to do their best to show their appreciation of everything. The Missis' baby, who had been tucked under her arm when we entered, had been annexed by one of the Sisters, who was an old friend, and in whose kindly arms baby sat beaming on the company.

Several of them were looking forward to a 'Sing-song' in the evening. 'We'll sing some songs for you, a real treat, Sister,' said the man who called attention to himself behind his plate, 'We'll have a real good time of it this evening, and after twelve o'clock we'll kick up a blooming row!' Whether the men thought the Sisters were going to sit in the 'kip' kitchen, singing with the men till after midnight, I don't know, but I pictured to myself the astonishment of the policeman on beat, who should look to see what the hilarious noise meant, and find the two Sisters in the midst of it! I thought the gentleman must have been a little bit 'on' to deliver his soul of these sentiments. Anyhow, the Missis cut in with, 'Now, you gentlemen, you as *can* sing must stop after tea and sing, for the Sisters are coming again; as for the drunks, you may go out.' The Missis and the caretaker allow no intoxicating drinks inside the house on any pretence. Of course, if the men drink outside, they have no control over that, but they are expected to behave themselves when they come in, or, if they don't, the Missis 'slings them out' herself. She is a little, delicate-looking, pretty woman, only twenty-four, but she has them well in hand, and makes them mind. We left when they were well on with the feeding, promising to look in again at seven o'clock.

Letter to
Miss Mary Boyle

CHARLES DICKENS

*The Victorian age was the heyday of the Christmas
pantomine. In this letter written on 28 December 1860,
Dickens tells of a mishap with scenery during a pantomine
at Covent Garden.*

I pass my time here (I am staying here alone) in working,
taking physic, and taking a stall at the Theatre every night.
On Boxing Night I was at Covent Garden. A dull pantomine
was 'worked' (as we say) better than I ever saw a heavy piece
worked on a first night, until suddenly and without a
moment's warning, every scene on that immense stage fell over
on its face, and disclosed Chaos by Gaslight behind! There
never was such a business – about sixty people who were on the
stage being extinguished in the most remarkable manner. Not
a soul was hurt. In the uproar, some mooncalf rescued a porter
pot, six feet high (one of which the clown had been drinking
when the accident happened), and stood it on the cushion of
the lowest Proscenium Box, P.S., beside a lady and
gentleman, who were dreadfully ashamed of it. The moment
the House knew that nobody was injured, they directed their
whole attention to this gigantic porter pot in its genteel
position (the lady and gentleman trying to hide behind it), and

The Play – The Play is the Thing by Augustus E. Mulready

roared with laughter. When a modest footman came from behind the curtain to clear it, and took it up in his arms like a Brobdingnagian Baby, we all laughed more than ever we had laughed in our lives. I don't know why . . .

The poor actors waylay me in Bow Street to represent their necessities; and I often see one cut down a court when he beholds me coming – cut round Drury Lane to face me – and come up towards me near this door in the freshest and most accidental way; as if I was the last person he expected to see on the surface of this globe. The other day, there thus appeared before me (simultaneously with a scent of rum in the air) one aged and greasy man, with a pair of pumps under his arm. He said he thought if he could get down to somewhere (I think it was Newcastle), he would get 'taken on' as Pantaloon, the existing Pantaloon being 'a stick, sir – a mere muff.' I observed that I was sorry times were so bad with him. 'Mr Dickens, you know our profession, Sir – no one knows it better, Sir – there is no right feeling in it. I was Harlequin on your own circuit, Sir, for five-and-thirty years, and was displaced by a boy, Sir – a boy!'

from

Journal to Stella

JONATHAN SWIFT

Dean Swift, poet, critic, brilliant political pamphleteer, and one of the greatest satirists in the English language, lived most of his life in Dublin where he was given the livings of four parishes near Dublin. However in 1710 he came to London for four years from where he wrote at regular fortnightly intervals to Esther Johnson (Stella) in Ireland, between whom there was a deep mutual affection. The journals are a vivid picture of his life and thoughts

· *A London Christmas* ·

*while residing in London and reveal his growing disen-
chantment with Whig policies and increasing allegiance to
the Tory Party.*

London, Dec. 24, 1711. I went into the City today in a coach,
and dined there. My cold is going. It is now bitter hard frost,
and has been so these three or four days . . . My lord
privy-seal set out this day for Holland: he'll have a cold
journey. I gave Patrick half a crown for his Christmas-box, on
condition he would be good, and he came home drunk at
midnight. I have taken a memorandum of it; because I never
design to give him a groat more. 'Tis cruel cold.

25. I wish MD a merry Christmas, and many a one; but mine
is melancholy: I durst not go to church today, finding myself a
little out of order, and it snowing prodigiously, and freezing.

27. The frost still continues violently cold. Mrs Masham
invited me to come tonight and play at cards; but our society
did not part till nine. But I supped with Mrs Hill, her sister,
and there was Mrs Masham and lord treasurer, and we stayed
till twelve. He is endeavouring to get a majority against next
Wednesday, when the House of lords is to meet, and the
Whigs intend to make some violent addresses against a Peace,
if not prevented. God knows what will become of us.

29. Saturday night. I have broke open my letter, and tore it
into the bargain, to let you know that we are all safe; the queen
has made no less than twelve lords to have a majority; and has
turned out the Duke of Somerset. She is awaked at last, and so
is lord treasurer: I want nothing now but to see the duchess [of
Marlborough] out. We are all extremely happy. Give me joy,
sirrahs. This is written in a coffee-house. Three of the new
lords are of our Society.

Schoolchildren coming home to London

30. The duke of Marlborough was at Court today, and nobody hardly took notice of him.

31. Our frost is broken since yesterday, and it is very slabbery; yet I walked into the city and dined, and ordered some things with the printer. . . . I hear the Duke of Marlborough is turned out of all his employments: I shall know tomorrow, when I am to carry Dr King to dine with the secretary.

January 1, 1712. Now I wish my dearest little MD many happy New-years; yes, both Dingley and Stella, aye, and Presto too, many happy new-years.

Yuletide

JOHN DAVIDSON

John Davidson was born in Scotland and began his working life as a teacher. However, in 1889 he gave up teaching and decided to head for London to make a living from journalism and short story writing. Though he was never rich he was able to enjoy the London social scene and club life, and eventually became best known as a master of narrative lyrical ballads. At first he had great sympathy for the poverty of the working classes of London – a sympathy which made him study their speech and adapt it for the purposes of his poetry; later, however, he became exasperated by their pessimism and lack of will to motivate themselves. He moved to Cornwall from London in 1908 only to commit suicide a year later by drowning.

Now wheel and hoof and horn
In every street
Stunned to its chimney-tops,
In every murky street –
Each lamp-lit gorge by traffic rent
Asunder,
Ravines of serried shops
By business tempests torn –
In every echoing street,
From early morn
Till jaded night falls dead,

Wheel, hoof, and horn
Tumultuous thunder
Beat
Under
A noteless firmament
Of lead.

When the winds list
A fallen cloud
Where yellow dregs of light
Befouled remain,
The woven gloom
Of smoke and mist,
The soot-entangled rain
That jumbles day and night
In city and town,
An umber-emerald shroud
Rehearsing doom,
The London fog comes down.
But sometimes silken beams,
As bright
As adamant on fire,
Of the uplifted sun's august attire,
With frosty fibrous light
Magnetic shine
Of happier dreams
That abrogate despair,
When all the sparkling air
Of smoke and sulphur shriven,
Like an iced wine
Fills the high cup
Of heaven;
For urban park and lawn,
The city's scenery,

· *A London Christmas* ·

Heaths, commons, dells
That compass London rich
In greenery,
With diamond-dust of rime
Empowdered, flash
At dawn;
And tossing bells
Of stealthy hansoms chime
With silvery crash
In radiant ways
Attuned and frozen up
To concert pitch –
In resonant ways,
Where wheels and hoofs inwrought,
Cars, omnibuses, wains,
Beat, boom, and clash
Discordant fugal strains
Of cymbals, trumpets, drums;
While careless to arrive,
The nerved pedestrian comes
Exulting in the splendour overhead,
And in the live
Elastic ground,
The pavement, tense and taut,
That yields a twangling sound
At every tread.

from

The Great Snow: A Dialogue

Written 'in a plaine Familiar Talke betweene a London Shopkeeper and a North-Country-Man', this dialogue refers to 'the cold Yeare' of 1614: 'in which men and cattell have perished to the generall losse of Farmers, Grasiers, Husbandmen, and all sorts of People in the Countrie: and no less hurtfull to citizens'. It shows that the great divide between north and south, city and country, was even greater then than it is today. In an earlier part of the dialogue, not printed here, the Citizen has to correct the North Countryman's view that in London 'all the angels of the kingdom, fly up and down here'. The general message is that country life is far healthier than life in the city, with people eating beef and bacon to make them strong, rather than fat, and using herbs from the garden, rather than wasting money on 'apothecaries'.

Nor. But I beseech you tell me, are all those news current, which we hear in the country:

Cit. What are they pray?

Nor. Marry sir, that your goodly river of Thames, (I call it yours, because you are a citizen; and because it is the nurse

Primrose Hill in Winter, a wood engraving by David Gentleman

that gives you milk and honey) is that (as 'tis reported) all frozen over again, that coaches run upon it?

Cit. No such matter.

Nor. When I heard it I prayed to God to help the fishes; it would be hard world with them, if their houses were taken over their heads. Nay sir, I heard it constantly affirmed, that all the youth of the city, did master upon it in battle array, one half against the other: and by my troth, I would have ambled on bare ten-toes a brace of hundred miles, to have such a triumph.

Cit. In sadness (I think) so would thousand besides yourself: but neither hath the river been this year (for all the vehement cold) so hard-hearted as to have such a glassy crusted floor; neither have our youth been up in arms in so dangerous a field: yet true it is, that the *Thames* began to play a few cold Christmas gambols; and that very children (in good array) great numbers, and with war-like furniture of drums, colours, pikes, and guns, (fit to their handling) have sundry times met army against army, in most of the fields about the city; to the great rejoicing of their parents, and numbers of beholders.

Nor. In good sooth I am sorry, I was not one of those standers by: I have been brought up as a scholar myself; and when I was young, our wars were wrangling disputations; but now it seems, that learning surfeits, having too many scholars; and that we shall need soldiers, when such young cockerels address to a battle: It shows like the *Epitome* of war; and it is a wonder for men to read it. Our painters in former ages have not drawn such pictures. But you cut me off from what I was about else to know.

Cit. What is that, father?

Nor. A bird came flying from the *North*, and chattered, that snow fell in such abundance within and round about the city of *London*, that none without could enter; nor any within, pass forth.

Cit. Fables, fables: a man may by the shadow have some guess how great the substance is: your own eye (upon your now being in *London*) can witness that your *Northern* song went to a wrong tune.

Nor. And yet by your favour, I think you have not seen your city so whited this forty years.

Cit. Indeed our Chronicles speak of one deep snow only, memorable to our time; and that was about 34 or 36 years ago.

Nor. Nay, not so much, but of your white bears, bulls, lions. &c., we had the description as fully as if with snow-balls in our hands, your apprentices and we silly country clowns had been at their baiting. I remember when I travelled into *Russia*, I have there seen white bears and white foxes: but some credulous fools would needs swear us down, that your city was full of such monsters; and that they ran alive in the streets, and devoured people: but I see your giants, and terrible herds of beasts, have done your city good service; for instead of grass, they have had cold provender, and helped to rid away the greater part of your snow.

Cit. They have indeed: and yet albeit an arm from heaven hath for several years, one after another, shaken whips over our land, sometimes scourging us with strange inundations of floods; then with merciless fires, destroying whole towns; then with intolerable and killing frosts, nipping the fruits of the earth: also for a long season, with scarcity of victuals, or in great plenty, sold exceedingly dear; and now last of all, with deep and most dangerous snows. Yet (as all the former laches), the prints being worn out, are forgotten; so of this, we make but a May-game, fashioning ridiculous monsters of that, which God in vengeance pours on our heads; when in doing so, we mock our own selves, that are more monstrous and ugly in all the shapes of sin.

Nor. You melt (Sir) out of a heap of snow, very profitable and wholesome instructions. But I suppose you have heard of some misfortunes, lately happening unto certain graziers:

Cit. No indeed, sir.

Nor. Then take it for truth and on my credit, that a good company of them coming up together to *London* with great store both of sheep and bullocks, they lost, by reason of the snows and deep waves, so many of either (especially of sheep) that perished in great numbers, even on the way, and before their faces, that if they had been sold to their value, it had been a sufficient estate to have maintained a very good man, and I have kept him rich all his life time.

Cit. I believe you: I pray sir, what is your opinion of this strange winter: give me your judgment I beseech you, of these frosts and snows; and what (in the school of your experience) you have read, or can remember, may be the effects, which

they may produce, or which of consequence are likely now to follow.

Nor. I shall do my best to satisfy you. When these great hills of snow, and these great mountains of ice be digged down, and be made level with the waters; when these hard rocks shall melt into rivers, and these white feathers of heaven stick upon the backs of floods; and that sudden thaws shall show, that the anger of these winter storms are mollified; then it is to be feared, that the swift, violent, and irresistable land-currents (or rather torrents) will bear down bridges, beat down buildings, overflow our corn-fields, overrun the pastures, drown our cattle, and endanger the lives both of man and beast, travelling on their way; and, unless God's hand of plenty be held open, a dearth, to strike the land in the following summer.

Cit. You say right. This prognostication which your judgment thus looks into, did always fall out to be true.

Nor. These extraordinary fevers (shaking a whole kingdom) have always other mortal diseases waiting upon them.

Cit. We are best to fear it; and by fearing, provide against them.

Nor. I pray God (at whose command the sun sends forth his heat, and the winds bitter storms to deface the fruits of it), that in this last affliction sent down in flakes from the angry element, all other miseries may be hidden, swallowed, and confounded.

Cit. I gladly, and from my heart, play the clerk, crying, *Amen.*

The Excellence of a London Christmas

THOMAS NORTH

Excess and over-indulgence has long been associated with Christmas celebrations, and the amount consumed at the Christmas table in both town and country has periodically provoked comment. An Elizabethan, Philip Massinger, said this of rural and civic appetites: 'Men may talk of country Christmases — their thirty-pound buttered eggs, their pies of carps' tongues, their pheasants drenched with ambergris, the carcases of three fat wethers brusied for gravy to make sauce for a single peacock; yet their feasts were fasts, compared with the city's.'

On 9 January 1731 Mr Thomas North described in Read's Weekly Journal *the marvellous hospitality and extensive fare he had received in London at the house of a friend.*

It was the house of an eminent and worthy merchant, and tho', sir, I have been accustomed in my own country to what may very well be called good housekeeping, yet I assure you I should have taken this dinner to have been provided for a

After the pudding

whole parish, rather than for about a dozen gentlemen: 'Tis impossible for me to give you half our bill of fare, so you must be content to know that we had turkies, geese, capons, puddings of a dozen sorts more than I had ever seen in my life, besides brawn, roast beef, and many things of which I know not the names, minc'd pyes in abundance, and a thing they call plumb pottage, which may be good for ought I know, though it seems to me to have 50 different tastes. Our wines were of the best, as were all the rest of our liquors; in short, the God of plenty seemed to reign here, and to make everything perfect, our company was polite and every way agreeable; nothing but mirth and loyal healths went round. If a stranger were to have made an estimate of London from this place, he would imagine it not only the most rich but the most happy city in the world.

from

Essays in London 1893

HENRY JAMES

*James's love of London began at the age of twelve when his
father brought the family over from America on a tour of
Europe. Later he described the capital as 'the biggest
aggregation of human life – the most complete compendium
of the world.' He even relished the thick fogs and the
persistent drizzle.*

There is still something that recalls to me the enchantments of
children – the anticipation of Christmas, the delight of a
holiday walk – in the way the shop-fronts shine into the fog. It
makes each of them seem a little world of light and warmth,
and I can still waste time in looking at them with dirty
Bloomsbury on one side and dirtier Soho on the other. There
are winter effects, not intrinsically sweet, it would appear,
which somehow, in absence, touch the chords of memory and
even the fount of tears: as for instance the front of the British
Museum on a black afternoon, or the portico, when the
weather is vile, of one of the big square clubs in Pall Mall. I
can give no adequate account of the subtle poetry of such

152

Sounds of Revelry by Augustus E. Mulready

reminiscences; it depends upon associations of which we have often lost the thread. The wide colonnade of the Museum, its symmetrical wings, the high iron fence in its granite setting, the sense of the misty halls within, where all the treasures lie – these things loom patiently through atmospheric layers which instead of making them dreary impart to them something of a cheer of red lights in a storm. I think the romance of a winter afternoon in London arises partly from the fact that, when it is

153

not altogether smothered, the general lamplight takes this hue of hospitality. Such is the colour of the interior glow of the clubs in Pall Mall, which I positively like best when the fog loiters upon their monumental staircases.

from

The Great Snow

RICHARD JEFFERIES

Richard Jefferies was born in Wiltshire in 1848, and although he came to London to take up a literary career, he remained pre-occupied with mainly rural themes. He disliked London and blamed it for his severe ill health. Perhaps not surprisingly, the fictional work The Great Snow *(which he described as 'an alternative catastrophe') has a distinctly apocalyptic tone.*

Much difficulty was experienced in locomotion. Trains were delayed but there was no interruption of the service, for the wind being still, there was no drift. All day and night of the 17th, 18th, 19th, and 20th the snow came steadily down, and on the 21st, despite all efforts to clear it, was 27 inches deep. Traffic in the streets was now suspended, and the steamers ceased to ply, partly from want of passengers, and partly

A Merry Christmas and A Happy New Year in London 1824

because of the dangerous obscurity. Most of the lines were blocked, and on the 22nd when the snow had an even depth of 33 inches, not a train reached London. Business was at an end. Till now the snow had been treated as a good joke by the populace who pelted each other in high spirits at their holiday, but when the trains ceased to arrive a species of desponding stupor seemed to fall upon them. The 23rd was a windy day, the breeze increasing from the east, till in the evening it blew almost hurricane. The grains of frozen snow lifted up and driven by the wind rushed up the streets like pellets from a gun. The narrow portals of Temple Bar were impassable, so vehement was the blast, and those who attempted to get through describe the hard snow as cutting the skin of their faces in a painful manner. This gale drifted the snow in huge mounds. On the morning of the 24th the western side of Trafalgar Square was 18 feet deep in snow, the entrance to the Haymarket was blocked up, and Regent Street near the Quadrant was buried under more than 20 feet. The Thames Embankment was quite clear – the wind having an unin-terrupted sweep up it – but the Houses of Parliament formed a dam across the stream of snow and against the eastern side there rose a mound at least 27 feet high. The fleet of merchantmen at the mouth of the Thames were driven on shore, and the whole northern and eastern coasts were strewn with wreckage. Many of these incidents were not ascertained till long afterwards, for the telegraph posts were blown down, the wires snapped, and all communication at an end. The bitter wind lasted five days, and is described as causing an insupportable cold which neither walls, nor curtains, nor roaring fires could overcome. It penetrated through every-thing. Smith says in his journal: 'We cowered round the fire, but could get no heat. We dragged our beds downstairs, and arranged them in a semi-circle round the fireplace on the carpet. Behind these we placed chairs hung with a screen of